THE WARRIOR BRIDE

God's Kingdom Advancing Through Spiritual Warfare

Jeanne Metcalf©2021

Cëgullah Publishing
International Copyright © 2022
www.cegullahpublishing.ca
All rights reserved

International Copyright © 2021
Jeanne Metcalf, Author
All rights reserved.

Textbook: ISBN 978-1-926489-42-1
Workbook: ISBN 978-1-926489-41-4

All scripture quotes originate from KJV[1], public domain. However, the name of God appears as YeHoVaH, not LORD. See appendix for more information.

Cover photo ©istock.com
Cover design by Jeanne Metcalf.

---

[1]KJV refers to all humankind as "man". Unless the passage itself refers to a particular male person, apply the message to all humankind, regardless of gender.

COPYRIGHT MATTERS

This book is an original manuscript by the author, protected by international copyright laws of Canada. Therefore, none of this author's work may be reproduced, in part or in whole, or stored in a retrieval system, or transmitted in any form or by any means, electronic, mechanical, photocopied, recorded or otherwise for commercial use without the *prior written* permission of the author. However, it is possible to receive permission to use short quotations for personal use, or use in a group study, or for permission to copy certain passages, or to make portions of the writings available for overhead viewing. Simply, contact the author[2] to request it.

SCRIPTURE MATTERS

All scripture quotes originate from KJV[3], public domain. However, the name of God appears as YeHoVaH, not LORD. See appendix for more information.

---

[2] To contact author, see *Contact Page in Appendix*

[3] KJV refers to all humankind as "man". Unless the passage itself refers to a particular male person, apply the message to all humankind, regardless of gender.

Dedication

In every generation since Adam, God calls for a people which, in accordance with His plan, *will love Him with all their heart, mind, soul and strength, and additionally, love their neighbour as themselves.*

All who answer and fulfill that call make up
His Bride.
To these I dedicate this book.

Additionally, I pray that God gives His strength, power and might to His Bride as her behaviour aligns with the Words and Ways of the Almighty. May the verbal and outward expression of her[4] corporate faith advance the Kingdom of God, reach the fullest possible potential *in their generation*, and thus, see His Heart rejoice and His Name glorified.

---

[4] As you read about the Bride, keep in mind that the word "Bride" speaks figuratively of "all believers" regardless of gender.

This is the Holy name of the God of Abraham, Isaac and Jacob, the God of Israel. We believe in honouring that sacred name. Therefore, to honour our God, we speak His Name aloud with reverence and respect Thus, you will see YeHoVaH[5] used consistently throughout this book.

"Let the heaven and earth praise him, the seas, and everything that moves therein. For God will save Zion, and will build the cities of Judah: that they may dwell there, and have it in possession. The seed also of his servants shall inherit it: and they that love his name shall dwell therein.
Psalm 69: 34-36

---

[5] For more information about the name of יהוה please see the Appendix.

INDEX

SECTION I:
THE BRIDE IDENTIFIED

Chapter	Title	Page
1	His Bride Envisioned……………	11
2	His Bride Defined………………..	23
3	His Bride's Creed………………..	45
4	His Bride's Warfare……………..	59

SECTION 2:
Part 1: THE BRIDE MOBILIZED

Part 1: To Love our God

5	His Weaponry of His Worship…	75
6	His Weaponry of His Name……	93
7	His Weaponry of His Word…….	107
8	His Weaponry of His Oneness…	121
9	His Weaponry of His Authority..	135
10	His Weaponry of His Dominion..	149

Part 2: To Love Our Neighbour

11	His Weaponry of His Gospel.…...	169
12	His Weaponry of His Coming….	187

Part 3: To Love Ourselves

13	His Weaponry of His Purity……	203
14	His Weaponry of His Seasons….	217

APPENDIX

About the King James Version.............	252
About the Author...............................	257
A Jewish Wedding Betrothal...............	31
Mount Sinai Wedding Betrothal...........	32
A Name to Honour...........................	235
Contact Information..........................	258
Other Books by this Author................	250
Salvation Message............................	243
Sinner's Prayer & Commitment...........	247
Scripture Index................................	254
The Bride's Creed.............................	58

SECTION 1

THE BRIDE IDENTIFIED

1

HIS BRIDE ENVISIONED

*And the Spirit and the **Bride** say, Come. And let him that heareth say, Come. And let him that is athirst come. And whosoever will, let him take the water of life freely.*

Revelation 22:17

Many years ago, as I rested in my bed, YeHoVaH awakened me. Upon awakening, my spiritual eyes saw an amazing thing. There, in front of me and walking towards me, came the most beautiful Bride. While her radiant garment shone brighter than the sun, a more dazzling beauty came from within. Overwhelming love, overpowering goodness and great mercy streamed from her being like sunbeams cutting through window glass in the early morning sun.

As this Bride walked closer to me, I heard words of praise for YeHoVaH sung to a heavenly tune, the likes of which no mortal ever sang. The

CHAPTER 1
His Bride Envisioned

Bride was singing. Closer and closer she came. With every step she took forward, my inner most being stirred with reverential emotion for her. I could see her. I could hear her, yet I was part of her! Over 20 years earlier, YeHoVaH redeemed me and made me His own, through the blood of His Only Begotten Son, Yeshua. I knew God considered believers His Bride, but it seemed a mystery to me, which I never really pursued Him to understand.

As I gazed at this amazing sight before my eyes, I wondered at the fundamental essence of her beauty. Was it her gentle facial expression or her eyes of love? Was it her compassion and mercy which shone through her clothing? Perhaps, in my eyes, I felt the atmosphere of holiness that radiated repentance wherever she walked. That touched me, deeply. Yet one thing stood out above all her attributes that I will never forget! Her powerful ability to affect every living soul who saw her pass by. That impact almost took my breath away, yet there came even more!

As I continued to watch her move forward, first, I noted those who rejoiced with her and decided to join her on the journey. These threw away

THE WARRIOR BRIDE
Advancing God's Kingdom Through Warfare

their former dreams and goals for those of greater value. However, not all thought like these people. I noticed many did not appreciate her nor her ways. Many hated her, deciding to become her adversary, some quickly, some over a period of time. Those who found her disagreeable, adverse to their goals and passions, hurled rocks, stones, and angry words of disgust at her. Yet, she never took cover, hid, nor disengaged her gaze from the Living One to Whom she served. Instead, forgiveness arose from deep within as she continued her constant praise and petitions to her Betrothed. In this, she fulfilled a portion of scripture written in the Psalms:

> Psalm 109:4
> For my love they are my adversaries: but I give myself unto prayer.

Death threats surrounded her, yet she focused beyond her mortality[6], caring not for the things of this world. Her composure remained in a steadfast gaze on her God, with her chorus of praise rising like incense before the throne in heaven. Intently, she waited for a revelation of His will. This became her directive. That

---

[6] Same mindset as Hebrews 11:13-16

CHAPTER 1
His Bride Envisioned

directive, both supernatural and supreme, saw its fulfillment with her every step.

Looking more intently, I saw the amazing essence of this Bride. Her unity of oneness with the Holy Spirit and the saints of all the ages, past, present and future flowed together to make her one amazing creation. Comprised of true believers, her voice echoed with faith, lifestyle declarations projecting a perfect, living example of Hebrews Chapter 11[7].

Still, there was more to see, for as she walked forward, lovingly touching the lives of others around her, an invisible realm appeared. Grave darkness tried to overcome her as an adversary moved with a mighty force to annihilate her. Earlier traps and snares, which that adversary set for her, she skillfully maneuvered to avoid them. As these failed, this adversary came with a greater force, pressing hard against her.

Suddenly, her gaze altered. Those gentle eyes which, earlier, looked upward to her Betrothed, and lovingly upon the children of men, unexpectedly changed. Her eyes became flames

---

[7] This Chapter is known as "The Faith Hall of Fame", refers to heroes of the faith.

of fire as she recognized that adversary lurking in the darkness. When he pressed forward, out of her mouth came a double-edged sword, as she spurted out scripture after scripture.

Her trust was in her Beloved. Her confrontation, backed by YeHoVaH's Word and power, hit sharp and direct. The adversary fled away, pulling back with dread. Strongholds broke. Chains fell off. Captives came running out of prison houses, embracing her extended hand, grateful to the battle won by a gentle giant with the fire of YeHoVaH alive and moving within her. This was her warrior side, in which former captives rejoiced.

Her shield, although invisible to my eyes, continued to repel every fiery dart her adversary threw at her. Victoriously, keeping her eyes focused on her future Husband, she responded just like Him. Her oneness with Him, in heart and soul, manifested in her deeds, as she sought to set the captives free. She knew His heart. She knew His goals. She knew His mandate. Her time preparing for her future she spent learning and doing the things that delighted His heart the most. Indeed, she

CHAPTER 1
His Bride Envisioned

readied herself to be His delightful companion for Eternity.

In seeing these things, I thought to myself, "this must be how YeHoVaH sees His Bride!" "This must be a prophetic glimpse of the reality of the destiny He perceives His Betrothed to fulfil." As I watched her continue on her way, increasing in the fire of God within, I felt overwhelmed at such greatness. Then, almost as quickly as she came, she vanished away from sight.

In that one moment in time, YeHoVaH pulled back a veil to reveal His concept of His beautiful Bride. I wondered *why He decided to do that*. Soon the answer became apparent, for almost immediately, the Spirit trumpeted out these words: "A calling out for the Ekklesia. Come out of the world, My People. Be holy as I am holy." That quick snippet of time revealed His Bride, showing that she had eyes for Him, and Him alone!

Through this scene, I perceived the dedication, love and modelling of His character, including His mighty warring side. Understanding His passion to redeem humankind, she willingly

THE WARRIOR BRIDE
Advancing God's Kingdom Through Warfare

engaged in spiritual warfare. She knew others need to know Him! Others need to experience His love, mercy and grace. They need an opportunity to enjoy the life He planned for them.

This warring side, neither violent nor aggressive toward humankind, pointed directly to the true spiritual source. With straight forward, dynamic, and authoritative commands, she took to task the evil entity who lived to rob, kill and destroy. Against that spiritual realm, she drew her sword! Her purpose in engaging in spiritual warfare produced fruit for her Beloved, as she saw His kingdom advance, touching the lives of those oppressed by ha satan[8].

This Bride, beautiful yet warring, intricately connected with her Betrothed. She exhibited a Godly authority, power and holiness, motivated and directed by the power of the Holy Spirit. She clung to her Betrothed's values and lived to fulfill them. She looked to Him, the One Who holds all things in His hands. She knew His anticipated response to her desires

---

[8] In Hebrew, ha satan means adversary.

CHAPTER 1
His Bride Envisioned

too, thus she fixed her eyes upon Him, praising Him *even when others threatened to destroy and annihilate her.*

This is the Bride as shown to me, but is this the Bride we know?

I believe we all agree, while this is a scriptural demonstration of His Bride, in reality, this is not *today's Betrothed!* However, it could be, especially, if we consider this the goal, and take the advice of the Holy Spirit to get there. Remember at the vision end He said, *"A calling out for the Ekklesia. Come out of the world, My People. Be holy as I am holy."* This is the major key to unlock the necessary changes to become that Betrothed, which delights the heart of the heavenly Bridegroom.

If this vision touched your heart in the same manner as it touched mine, then, together, let us have a heart-to-heart talk with YeHoVaH. Let us tuck beneath the wings of the Living God to learn how that vision becomes a reality in the here and now, as each one of us does our part. As we take God's holy hand extended and allow the light of the Holy Spirit to penetrate deep within, let us stay in that place of abiding. Let us see the removal, in our own lives, of every part of the "world" as YeHoVaH defines it. Let us truly embrace God's ideal of holiness so that we, indeed, become holy as He is holy.

In addition, let us learn how to move in the power of that beautiful Betrothed of YeHoVaH, affecting the world around us with a greater, more intense power that changes lives. For many, that means embracing a different vision of the Bride, namely, **her warrior side.** It means coming to terms with the existence of a realm beyond the natural eyes of man.

It means acknowledging, as the Word teaches, that the powers of darkness exist and not figuratively. Rather, let us see them as an entity with which we must contend **and overrule.** No matter how we define it, people, saved and unsaved unlike, face invisible foes on a regular basis. Therefore, let us learn to contend with those powers of darkness as Yeshua did with fire in our eyes and a two-edged sword *(His Word)* in our mouths.

With His strength, wisdom and power, moving in tune with His Holy Spirit, let us push back the adversary, ha satan. Let us wreck and

CHAPTER 1
His Bride Envisioned

destroy ha satan's strongholds. Let us use the Word of God in such a manner as to break chains and see captives set free. By the power and the direction of the Holy Spirit, let us see God's kingdom advance through God-inspired and God-directed spiritual warfare.

Dear Reader, it is my prayer that we always remember and function as the gentle giant, a friend and ally to humankind. Yet, we must engage in another side, *waging war in defense of humankind against the spiritual forces of darkness.* In that way, oppressing forces of darkness retreat; bronze doors open before us. Then, as the ekklesia, we operate as the anointed of YeHoVaH should:

Isaiah 45:1-3
> 1 ¶ Thus saith YeHoVaH to his anointed, to Cyrus, whose right hand I have holden, to subdue nations before him; and I will loose the loins of kings, to open before him the two leaved gates; and the gates shall not be shut; 2 I will go before thee, and make the crooked places straight: I will break in pieces the gates of brass, and cut in sunder the bars of iron: 3 And I will give thee the treasures of darkness, and hidden

riches of secret places, that thou mayest know that I, YeHoVaH, which call [thee] by thy name, [am] the God of Israel.

While this message found fulfillment in Cyrus, nevertheless, it holds a powerful message to all God calls to advance His Kingdom, including His beloved Bride[9]. Such a directive calls to all, who are part of the Bride, to become a spiritual nightmare to ha satan and his forces. Pushing back these forces, while not a pleasant task, results in an open door for others to escape torment and walk through a wide-open door to know God's Promised freedom!

Indeed, in looking at the Bride YeHoVaH presented to me, and in measuring her every function with the Word of God, *I see a need for a gentle giant, who also functions as a warrior!*

Do you?

If you agree, come along on a journey to discover God's Bride as shown in His Word. As we explore scripture, you'll discover direct passages, as well as some powerful prophetic

---

[9] Keep in mind that within this book, the term "Bride" is figurative and not gender specific.

CHAPTER 1
His Bride Envisioned

pictures, which relate a picture of the Bride showing both the gentle giant and warrior. If open to the voice of the Holy Spirit, the result should encourage each believer to see, learn and take an active part in the whole behaviour of the Bride, including that forgotten side of

"The Warrior Bride".

Luke 4:18-19
"18 The Spirit of YeHoVaH [is] upon me, because he hath anointed me to preach the gospel to the poor; he hath sent me to heal the broken-hearted, to preach deliverance to the captives, and recovering of sight to the blind, to set at liberty them that are bruised, 19 To preach the acceptable year of YeHoVaH."

Please note: the word **"Bride"**, when referring to the Betrothed of God, means the corporate gathering of all true believers, *regardless of gender*.

HIS BRIDE DEFINED

"Fear not; for thou shalt not be ashamed: neither be thou confounded; for thou shalt not be put to shame: for thou shalt forget the shame of thy youth, and shalt not remember the reproach of thy widowhood any more. For thy Maker [is] thine husband; YeHoVaH of hosts [is] his name; and thy Redeemer the Holy One of Israel; The God of the whole earth shall he be called."

Isaiah 54:4-5

It seems confusion exists regarding the full identity of the Bride. Many New Testament believers classify the Bride's identity as comprised of all born again saints. Some include Israel into the identity, while others do not. Recently, a new theory came into existence, describing one Bride for the Father, namely Israel, and one Bride of the Son, namely the

CHAPTER 2
His Bride Defined

church. This new theory of two Brides, scripture does not support for it speaks of but *one Bride!*

**Who is that Bride?
Is she figurative?
Is she a combination of believers, both Jew and Gentile?
Or, as declared in the book of Revelation, is the Bride a beloved city?**

Revelation 21: 9-10

> 9 ¶ And there came unto me one of the seven angels which had the seven vials full of the seven last plagues, and talked with me, saying, Come hither, I will shew thee the bride, the Lamb's wife. 10 And he carried me away in the spirit to a great and high mountain, and shewed me that great city, the holy Jerusalem, descending out of heaven from God,

This scripture, like all comparisons in the Word, depends on the purpose God employs the comparison. Comparisons, after all, exist to help the natural mind of man understand spiritual truths. This Lamb's wife, the city as spoken about in Revelation 21:9-10, presents a powerful truth regarding the heavenly city,

Jerusalem, the future place of residence where believers dwell, along with the One Whose brightness lights the city.

However, to define the Bride as scripture depicts her, we need to look at both the Hebraic and Apostolic[10] scriptures. To do so, we will begin at the Exodus of the children of Israel from Egypt, doing a quick review of their encounter with YeHoVaH at the base of Mt. Sinai.

AT THE BASE OF MOUNT SINAI

As the children of Israel arrived at the base of Mount Sinai, God arranges to commune with them. He invites them to become His people. In Jewish terms, God invites them to become His Cegullah, His special Jewel, His Beloved or in other words *His Bride*. We see that in the following scripture:

> Exodus 19:1-6
> 1 In the third month, when the children of Israel were gone forth out of the land of Egypt, the same day came they [into] the

---

[10] Hebraic scriptures are those written between Adam and Yeshua's coming. Apostolic scriptures are those written after Yeshua's coming.

CHAPTER 2
His Bride Defined

wilderness of Sinai. 2 For they were departed from Rephidim and were come [to] the desert of Sinai and had pitched in the wilderness; and there Israel camped before the mount. 3 And Moses went up unto God, and YeHoVaH called unto him out of the mountain, saying, Thus shalt thou say to the house of Jacob, and tell the children of Israel;

4 Ye have seen what I did unto the Egyptians, and [how] I bare you on eagles' wings, and brought you unto myself. *5 Now therefore, if ye will obey my voice indeed, and keep my covenant, then ye shall be a peculiar treasure* **(Cegullah[11])** *unto me above all people: for all the earth [is] mine:* 6 And ye shall be unto me a kingdom of priests, and an holy nation. These [are] the words which thou shalt speak unto the children of Israel.

To those familiar with Hebrew terms in ancient days, this word "Cegullah", translated as "peculiar treasure", while speaking of a precious jewel cherished by its owner,

---

[11] Strong's Concordance, Hebrew #5459 סְגֻלָּה cëgullah seg-ool-law', Peculiar treasure, special treasure, jewel.

additionally has further connotations. When speaking of human love, to express the feelings of a husband thoroughly enthralled with his wife, she is *His Cegullah!* With that thought in mind, we understand there is more in this passage of Exodus 19:5-6 than meets the eye. Here, at Mt. Sinai, God invited the people who came out of Egypt to become the Cegullah, the precious jewel of the living God. In other words, here is an invitation for Israel to become YeHoVaH's Bride.

This marriage, like marriages on earth, call for a oneness, a forsaking of all others, and a clinging to each other. In other words, only the same two people come together to consummate and then, operate the marriage. Fulfilling the marriage God designed demands total fidelity! In the case of God with His People, this fidelity requires a total forsaking of the former life before becoming His People. That forsaking included saying goodbye to all other gods, which they may have loved and served.

A marriage of God's people to God, reflects the same idea that Yeshua presented to His Disciples when He spoke about the unity or oneness in marriage:

CHAPTER 2
His Bride Defined

Mark 10:7-8
> 7 For this cause shall a man leave his father and mother and cleave to his wife; 8 And they twain shall be one flesh: so, then they are no more twain, but one flesh.

This oneness, shown here as the union of a husband and wife on earth, represents God's intentions with His People. As a Husband, God honours and cherishes His Bride, providing for her, keeping her, and her alone, as His Cegullah. The Bride, in turn, honours and cherishes her Husband, ensuring her faithfulness to Him never wanes. Thus, our understanding of the God-ordained marriage, helps us to grasp the heart of the message God desires to relate to us.

In Exodus, YeHoVaH portrayed Himself as a Husband, Who first ransomed His Bride out of the state of slavery. Tenderly, He carried her on Eagle's wings, away from her desolate and abusive state of slavery to a place of safety where He, Himself, would care for her. This Bride and Groom relationship of YeHoVaH with Israel, shows us the loyalty God expects to give as that which He expects to receive from His people.

THE WARRIOR BRIDE
Advancing God's Kingdom Through Warfare

This comparison of the marital relationship shows us but one aspect of our God, Who loves and cares for His People. Scripture gives us many additional examples of YeHoVaH's care, in other capacities, to broaden our understanding of Him. YeHoVaH presents Himself as a Father, as a Healer, as a Shepherd, as well as other capacities we understand, just so we can grasp more about Him.

Each comparison which He gives takes something of what we know and experience on earth and attaches it to an aspect of YeHoVaH's character so that we, His people know Him. In other words, even though God possesses qualities which range far above that of humankind's, nevertheless, He uses our lifestyle knowledge to help us grasp the behaviour of the invisible One.

Returning to the comparison of YeHoVaH as a husband, we see by examining Exodus 19 with a close eye, that YeHoVaH first brought Israel to Himself, and at the base of Mt. Sinai, invited her to become His Cegullah. Then, He proceeded to lay out certain aspects of what it takes to belong to Him. As we look at these events, which took place at the base of Mt. Sinai, we discover a strong comparison between those events and

CHAPTER 2
His Bride Defined

those of an ancient Jewish betrothal and wedding. [12]

To begin, let's examine the basic aspects of the ancient Jewish wedding, from betrothal to wedding consummation. In that way, you will discover some aspects of YeHoVaH's relationship with Israel, simply by looking at the scripture from another angle, using its cultural setting.

Here are two charts which give *highlights* of the ancient Jewish wedding, and some of the corresponding events at the base of Mt. Sinai.

---

[12] Much of the procedure still applies to Jewish weddings, today!

A JEWISH WEDDING BETROTHAL

1. Perspective husband chooses his bride[13]. His plan, of course, is to, eventually, remove her from her father's home and bring her to himself in the place he prepares for her.
2. Asks for her consent, however, should she refuse his proposal, the perspective groom looks elsewhere.
3. Before ceremony for betrothal begins, both perspective bride and groom use the mikvah (place of cleansing).
4. Ketubah[14] is written, terms agreed upon, and when finished, becomes a binding Covenant.
5. Groom goes away and prepares a home.
6. Bride prepares for her husband
7. Groom comes for his wife.
8. Celebration of marriage takes place under a Chuppah.

---

[13] Many dynamics go into this choice, including the arrangements with the bride's father. People, at that time, did not necessarily marry the woman they loved, rather, as the Jews relate to us, they loved the woman they married!

[14] Marriage terms, ensuring Bride's rights are respected, and outlines groom's treatment of her.

CHAPTER 2
His Bride Defined

MT SINAI WEDDING BETROTHAL
1. God chose a people for Himself (Exodus 19:1-5)
2. People give their consent (Exodus 19:7-8)
3. People spend time preparing for meeting with God (Exodus 19:10)
4. Ketubah[15] is prepared (Exodus 20:1-17) • Part A) Bride to be God's Cegullah. • Part B) Bride to obey and be His Nation. God *spoke the terms of the Ketubah verbally,* and *later wrote them* on the tablets of stone. (10 Commandments). Binding covenant made.
5. Thick clouds on mount acted like a Chuppah. Representatives came to eat & drink with God. (Exodus 24:10). Those invited guests return to the camp. Moses goes up on the Mount for 40 days and nights. YeHoVaH writes the 10 commandments in stone, a written Ketubah for His Bride.

---

[15] A Ketubah outlines the marriage terms.

Here, we will stop, because the remainder of the points see their fulfillment at a latter point in time.

In the scenario of Mt. Sinai, Moses returns to the mountain top to spend time with YeHoVaH. Moses' absence effected the Bride in such a manner as to become unfaithful to YeHoVaH.

Without the bodily presence of Moses, the Betrothed makes a god for herself and worships it. This alters the completion of the remaining points, such as the marriage consummation. From the point of Israel's idolatry and onward, YeHoVaH keeps His role as the Betrothed of Israel, yet they forsake Him, time and time again.

THE FALLEN, IDOLATROUS BRIDE
Moses returns, from the mountain top with God to the camp below, where he finds the idolatry of Israel taking place. In anger, Moses breaks the tablets of stone, the written Ketubah. Israel, who earlier agreed to those terms, forsook their commitment.

Moses points out their sinful state and calls for a separation of people from their idol worship.

CHAPTER 2
His Bride Defined

Those who wish to follow God, Moses invites to stand by him. Then, Moses commands the death sentence to those who refuse. Three thousand people die that day.

With great disappointment, Moses returns to the mountain top to spend time with YeHoVaH, at which point, God commands Moses to write the 10 commandments on new stone tablets.[16] [17] Later, Moses returns to the people. They then build the Tabernacle in which God promises to dwell, which includes the sacrificial system, which God gave to Moses to provide atonement for the sins of the people. Surely, God promises to dwell amongst those who embrace a mindset of repentance and choose His call for a walk of holiness over and above the desires of the flesh.

YEHOVAH'S BRIDE
Looking again at this proposal to Israel and noting her verbal acceptance of YeHoVaH, we see Israel classified as His Bride; however, we must keep in mind that God continually dealt with their unfaithfulness. Israel, as YeHoVaH's Bride must learn to keep His commandments!

---

[16] Exodus 34:28
[17] The first tablets God wrote with His finger. The second, God commanded Moses to write.

THE WARRIOR BRIDE
Advancing God's Kingdom Through Warfare

She must learn to be faithful to Him. History shows God's constant call to her to do so, and His inevitable Hand of judgment when left with no choice.

However, God, at no point in time, forsook His commitment to His Bride. While He says, at a certain place in scripture, He turned His face away, He did so due to Israel's sin. Still, His heart and passion for her never waned. Israel was and always will be, YeHoVaH's Cegullah.

God never replaced Israel! How could anyone ever replace their Cegullah? Rather, the heart of God longed for His Beloved to recognize His love for them and return to Him with all their heart. Scripture shows that YeHoVaH's eyes remain focused on His Beloved Israel, longing for her return to Him.

To further understand about YeHoVaH's Bride, then, we must realize that Israel's exodus portrayed another prophetic picture. In analyzing the people who left Egypt we note that not all who exited were born of the seed of Jacob. According to many scholars, Jewish and otherwise, Gentiles comprised a part of the people of the Exodus. *Technically,* once they

CHAPTER 2
His Bride Defined

crossed through the Red Sea, passing over to the other side, they became Hebrews, which term means, "crossing over" or "from the other side". In other words, these Gentiles simply became part of Israel, and thus, were included in the invitation to be YeHoVaH's Cegullah.

Thus, to define the Bride of YeHoVaH, *one must, therefore, include all[18] who willingly, through their choice and behaviour, align with the God of Israel.* In other words, all who chose to follow YeHoVaH, the God of Abraham, Isaac and Jacob, cross over into a new way of life, included within the classification of God's people.

By fulfilling the required terms of the covenant agreement with YeHoVaH, *(part of which includes learning His Ways, and using a Mikvah, an immersion in the cleansing waters,)* by their choice and subsequent actions, they become part of His Cegullah, or part of His Bride. Thus, in summary, we see the Bride of YeHoVaH always included both Jew and Gentiles. Nothing has changed! It is so, today.

---

[18] "All" includes every born again believer (no matter their gender), who align their behaviour with YeHoVaH's requirements.

THE BRIDE'S MAIN FOCUS

A bride aims to embrace a oneness with her husband, while retaining her own identity, for surely, any good marriage gives room for the wife to possess her own uniqueness. As the bride lives out her life, utilizing her own God ordained uniqueness, her focus, yes, her every action, still has the possibility of reflecting a oneness with her husband. Any onlooker, when noticing a man's wife, should perceive through her behaviour and mention of her spouse, an open door to reveal her husband's ideals. Such a oneness the prophet Isaiah describes this way:

Isaiah 42:5-7
5 ¶ Thus saith God YeHoVaH, he that created the heavens, and stretched them out; he that spread forth the earth, and that which cometh out of it; he that giveth breath unto the people upon it, and spirit to them that walk therein: 6 I YeHoVaH have called thee in righteousness, and will hold thine hand, and will keep thee, and give thee for a covenant of the people, for a light of the Gentiles; 7 To open the blind eyes, to bring out the prisoners from the

CHAPTER 2
His Bride Defined

prison, [and] them that sit in darkness out of the prison house.

While this passage gives clear reference to the Messiah, it also addresses Israel's oneness with YeHoVaH. He called her in righteousness and for a righteous purpose. Her help to fulfill that purpose lies in remembering the One Who holds her hand and keeps her. She is a gift to the world as a covenant of the people, a light to the Gentiles! Blinded eyes open to see the reality of YeHoVaH through her ministry! Prisoners in jails, especially those sitting in great darkness, find release from their prison houses.

This well defines the goal of the Bride of God! She must be that Light for all to see! Her behaviour, goals and aspirations align with that of Her Husband and thus, she draws others to her husband. That drawing brings their freedom, and with it an invitation to become part of her, part of the Bride, part of what makes up His Cegullah.

ARE THERE TWO BRIDES OR ONE?
In our opening of this chapter, you read: "Recently, a new theory came into existence, describing one Bride for the Father, namely

Israel, and one Bride of the Son, namely the church. This new theory of two Brides, scripture does not support for it speaks of but *one Bride!* Who is that Bride? Is she figurative? Is she a combination of believers, both Jew and Gentile? "

QUESTION: If scripture speaks only of one Bride, how do we reconcile the fact that some teach there are two Brides: one for the Father, namely Israel, one for Yeshua, namely the church?

Those who hold to the two-Bride theory, additionally, often hold to the two-house theory, namely the Jewish house and the Gentile House. Some reasons, obviously, exist for these theories, however, one cannot separate either the First Covenant from the Second, nor the Father from the Son. Scripture teaches YeHoVaH is One:

John 14:6-10
> 6 Jesus saith unto him, I am the way, the truth, and the life: no man cometh unto the Father, but by me. 7 If ye had known me, ye should have known my Father also: and from henceforth ye know him and have

CHAPTER 2
His Bride Defined

seen him. 8 Philip saith unto him, Lord, shew us the Father, and it sufficeth us. 9 Jesus saith unto him, Have I been so long time with you, and yet hast thou not known me, Philip? he that hath seen me hath seen the Father; and how sayest thou [then], Shew us the Father? 10 Believest thou not that I am in the Father, and the Father in me? the words that I speak unto you I speak not of myself: but the Father that dwelleth in me, he doeth the works.

To see Yeshua, according to the words of Yeshua, is to see the Father. There is a oneness in the Godhead which believers cannot overlook. You cannot divide Yeshua from the Father, nor the Holy Spirit from Yeshua. God is One!

Deuteronomy 6:4
4 Hear, O Israel: YeHoVaH our God [is] one YeHoVaH:

Therefore, if YeHoVaH and Yeshua are one, ***there can only be one Bride!*** At Mount Sinai YeHoVaH invited all who willingly accepted Him as their only God to come, learn of His Ways, obey and walk with Him. Most of those who accepted were from the seed of Abraham, *however, Gentiles were among that number.* As a nation following His Word, obeying Him, and keeping Him as their only God, **they, thus, formed His Bride.**

Remember also, that when Yeshua came, He called Israel to return to the Father. He came as that open door, which repented sinners walk through to know *YeHoVaH*. Whoever will may come! Each believer, according to scripture, is baptized (mikvahed) into Yeshua[19]. Understanding and embracing Yeshua's oneness with the Father becomes paramount.

That oneness, once embraced, removes the necessity for people to even consider if Christian believers become one with Jewish believers. In Messiah, all are one! Nevertheless, scripture does address that problem, *indirectly*, through the words of the Apostle Paul in Romans Chapter 11.

Here Paul speaks of the oneness of the Olive tree. That olive tree stands as another illustration of the oneness of believers in

---

[19] That oneness in Yeshua, water baptism symbolizes.

CHAPTER 2
His Bride Defined

Yeshua! All are shown in scripture **as part of the Olive tree of Israel,** with natural branches and those engrafted. All within Yeshua, both Jew and Gentile, form the Bride. In other words, there is but one Bride comprised of both Jew and Gentile, *engrafted as one into Yeshua.*

Declaring the existence of two Brides does a great injustice to the unity of the Godhead. Remember:

Deuteronomy 6:4
4 Hear, O Israel: YeHoVaH our God [is] one YeHoVaH:

Furthermore, referring again to the theory of two Brides, that theory disassembles the point of the Apostle Paul speaking about the olive tree with its natural and engrafted branches. The oneness in Messiah is just that, a ONENESS!

Dear Reader, hopefully you conclude here, as scripture teaches, there is but one Bride! She is composed of the saints of all the ages, both Jew and Gentile, who chose to align with the God of Abraham, Isaac and Jacob, and as believers, live their lives before YeHoVaH's face, careful to walk within His Laws and commandments.

Whether these believers entered and kept their relationship with God through the first covenant, or entered through the shed blood of Yeshua, *does not matter*. What matters is how the Bride, *in each generation,* lives out her call, her mission, and her assignments from heaven.

Our job is <u>*not*</u> *to learn* to differentiate and separate the saints of the Living God, sorting through who came into covenant with God and when. It is enough that our God knows and understands that aspect of the Bride. Ours is to understand the Bride, today, learn her God-assigned goals and live them out under the power of the Holy Spirit. Ours is to be an effective and powerful part of the Bride in our generation!

**Are you ready for that assignment!
If so, read on!**

3

HIS BRIDE'S CREED

"But we are bound to give thanks always to God for you, brethren beloved of the Lord, because God hath from the beginning chosen you to salvation through sanctification of the Spirit and belief of the truth: Whereunto he called you by our gospel, to the obtaining of the glory of our Lord Jesus Christ. Therefore, brethren, stand fast, and hold the traditions which ye have been taught, whether by word, or our epistle.
2 Thessalonians 2:13-15

As God's Bride functions in her divinely ordained assignments, she must have a basis, or a creed by which to operate. A creed, in general terms, applies to an authoritative outline of values, which help one to function in their faith. Therefore, the Bride's Creed *summarizes* her required behaviour, which she lives out in the world. That creed, God gave to His Bride when He carved out the

CHAPTER 3
His Bride's Creed

10 commandments on the Mount. In effect, those 10 commandments stood as a basic outline, or bones of their required commitment to their Betrothed. Yeshua, as well as other prophets, **summarized those commandments**[20]:

> Matthew 22:37-40
> 37 Jesus said unto him, Thou shalt love the Lord thy God with all thy heart, and with all thy soul, and with all thy mind. 38 This is the first and great commandment. 39 And the second [is] like unto it, Thou shalt love thy neighbour as thyself. 40 On these two commandments hang all the law and the prophets.

This statement made by Yeshua, encapsulates the commandments of YeHoVaH and therefore stands as a good creed for the Bride. It represents all requirements necessary to fulfill her commitments towards God and humankind, giving, even, a reference to the way she treats herself. Wherever the Bride moves, this Creed, or rule of thumb, should motivate and guide her.

---

[20] For brevity here, we will use the words of Yeshua in the Creed, but one could also use the 10 commandments.

PREPARED FOR HER BETROTHED

Brides-to-be, today, as well as in days of old, focused on getting ready for their marriage. They gathered together whatever things the custom of the day required. Some items might incorporate special items, little extras such as special mementos, which help to operate the new household. When the bride entered the marriage home, in some culture, these things remained the bride's property, while in other cultures, it became either joint property or in ownership, at times, transferred to the husband.

As the bride, however, went about preparing for the marriage home, most tried to avoid things their future husband disliked. In the mind of most brides, the marriage home becomes their comfort zone, their little nest where each one enjoys their own personal space, as well as each other's company. Here, in this safe place, they carry on the normal functions of life.

YeHoVaH's Bride, in so many ways, is no different in that respect than other brides, in that she prepares for her marriage with the groom. However, YeHoVaH's Bride, like ancient Jewish brides, knows not the time nor

CHAPTER 3
His Bride's Creed

the hour of the wedding. It comes at some future unknown date[21]. In the meantime, between the time of the betrothal to her wedding day, just like the ancient Jewish bride, YeHoVaH's Bride must consider herself already married. Only a legal, written divorce could separate ancient Jewish marriages! With YeHoVaH, nothing breaks His commitment to His Bride! Thus, as YeHoVaH's Bride prepares for her wedding day, her focus must shift to serve Him and Him alone! She must learn to develop a single eye for her husband, living in a manner above that of the world, its desires, philosophies and principles.

As she lives out her life developing that single eye, she seeks to please Him in every way. She delights in what delights Him. That aspect of their relationship develops over time as the Bride gets to know Him. Due to YeHoVaH's invisibility, this aspect of getting to know Him happens without physical interaction, however, it does transpire through ability of the Holy Spirit. He teaches the Bride to know her

---

[21] In ancient days, no one knew the date of the wedding until it happened! The father, when he deemed it appropriate, gave the son permission to fetch his bride. Then, it all began!

THE WARRIOR BRIDE
Advancing God's Kingdom Through Warfare

Betrothed. This aspect of the relationship, as well as the betrothal and the journey, the Bible prophetically demonstrates in the Book of Genesis.

In Genesis Chapter 24, Abraham seeks a wife for his son, Isaac. So, Abraham calls his most faithful servant, Eliezer,[22] commanding him to go to country of Abraham's birth and from there bring back a wife for Isaac. Abraham specified that Isaac's bride must *not* be of Canaanite seed, but only of the kindred of Abraham. Also, the woman must willing to leave the land of her birth to live the wandering life with Isaac, as he lives out his life and inheritance within the promises of God. [23]

Eliezer, who has command of all his master's goods, takes what he needs and without hesitation, heads straight for Mesopotamia, unto the city of Nahor[24]. As Eliezer, his servants and the camels which he took with him arrive at

---

[22] We know the servant's name as the Bible records it in Genesis 15:2. However, in this story, the servant's name is not mentioned.
[23] Genesis 24:1-8
[24] Nahor begat Terah. Genesis 11:24 Terah begat Abram (Abraham) Genesis 11:26

CHAPTER 3
His Bride's Creed

their destination, Eliezer gets ready to give the camels a drink. He causes them to kneel down. It was eventide hour when the women of the village go out to draw water. Knowing this, Eliezer prays to YeHoVaH. He asked the following:

Genesis 24:13-14
13 Behold, I stand *here* by the well of water; and the daughters of the men of the city come out to draw water: **14** And let it come to pass, that the damsel to whom I shall say, Let down thy pitcher, I pray thee, that I may drink; and she shall say, Drink, and I will give thy camels drink also: *let the same be* she *that* thou hast appointed for thy servant Isaac; and thereby shall I know that thou hast shewed kindness unto my master.

Rebekah, a daughter of Abraham's brother, a virgin, and fair to look upon, arrives at the well with her pitcher upon her shoulder. She bends down, fills her pitcher, and then stands up again.

Genesis 24:17-20
17 And the servant ran to meet her, and said, Let me, I pray thee, drink a little water

of thy pitcher. **18** And she said, Drink, my lord: and she hasted, and let down her pitcher upon her hand, and gave him drink. **19** And when she had done giving him drink, she said, I will draw *water* for thy camels also, until they have done drinking. **20** And she hasted, and emptied her pitcher into the trough, and ran again unto the well to draw *water*, and drew for all his camels.

Eliezer, amazed and pleased by Rebekah's response to his request, says nothing. His mind wonders if YeHoVaH made this journey prosperous. He'd know that in a moment! After the woman finished drawing water for his camels, he gives her some expensive jewelry: a golden earring and two bracelets of gold. He asks about her lineage. He rejoices at her answer, for YeHoVaH, indeed, prospered his journey[25]. Here before him is God's choice of a bride for his master's son!

Eliezer, at Rebekah's invitation, goes to lodge with Rebekah's family. There Rebekah's family offers Eliezer food, however, he refuses to eat

---

[25] Genesis 24:21-25

CHAPTER 3
His Bride's Creed

until he completes his master's business. He speaks of the errand he received from Abraham. He rehearses his meeting with Rebekah, outlining how she fulfilled the conditions Eliezer gave to YeHoVaH to show which damsel YeHoVaH chose[26]. Rebekah's family, as they heard the story related to them, conclude that YeHoVaH, indeed, brought this about.

Due to Eliezer's insistence to expedite his journey, the family presents the marriage offer to Rebekah, which offer includes the bridal price[27]. She accepts.

Additionally, the servant Eliezer gives gifts to Rebekah's family. Then, with permissions in place and the bridal price paid, Eliezer takes Rebekah to meet Isaac.

> Genesis 24:59-61
> **59** And they sent away Rebekah their sister, and her nurse, and Abraham's servant, and his men. **60** And they blessed Rebekah, and said unto her, Thou *art* our sister, be thou *the mother* of thousands of millions, and let thy seed possess the gate

---

[26] Genesis 24:34b to 49

[27] This aspect we do not see directly, but indirectly as gifts were given to Rebekah's family.

of those which hate them. **61** And Rebekah arose, and her damsels, and they rode upon the camels, and followed the man: and the servant took Rebekah and went his way.

On this journey, as the servant leads the group back to Abraham, one wonders about the thoughts of Rebekah. Did she ask the servant to tell her about her future husband? This we are not told; however, human nature would probably indicate her inquiring, maybe even pestering Eliezer with questions.

In any case, in the evening as they arrive near their destination, they discover Isaac meditating in a field. Isaac sees the entourage coming. Rebekah, upon seeing him, inquires about him. She discovers this is her betrothed. Immediately, she covers herself with her veil, following a custom of her day.

Eliezer and the travellers with him, including Rebekah, meet Isaac. Eliezer relates all the events to Isaac. Isaac brings Rebekah into his tent and consummates the marriage[28].

---

[28] Genesis 24:62-67

CHAPTER 3
His Bride's Creed

Genesis 24:67

> **67** And Isaac brought her into his mother Sarah's tent, and took Rebekah, and she became his wife; and he loved her: and Isaac was comforted after his mother's *death*.

ANALYSIS OF THIS STORY

This wonderful story, in a delightful way, prophetically shows, a picture of the Bride of YeHoVaH on her journey to meet with her Betrothed. This prophetic picture, once understood, helps believers to grasp even more about the Heavenly Bride as she is courted and escorted by the Holy Spirit to her destiny.

THE SERVANT

Genesis 24 constantly and consistently refers to Eliezer, only as the "Servant".

> **Scripture does this to demonstrate the role of the Holy Spirit.**

As the servant leaves his master's house, he brings all the goods he needs with him to complete the assignment. This shows the availability of the Holy Spirit to all treasures of heaven, without restraint.

REBEKAH

Rebekah, in this story, represents the heavenly Bride[29], the choice of YeHoVaH, which comes from a lineage akin to Abraham. Additionally, Rebekah willingly forsakes all she knows to return with the servant to his country. She represents the Bride forsaking the goods of earth for the things of heaven. As Rebekah unites with Isaac, whom she never personally met, the Bride one day unites with her Betrothed. Also, in this picture, we see the gifts received by the Bride and the payment of the bridal price.

THE JOURNEY

As Rebekah, the servant and all parties disembark, they journey to the place where the Master lives. Their goal: *bring the virgin bride Rebekah, who had but a single eye towards Isaac, forward to her destiny.* Everyone on that journey focused on fulfilling that task. No one quit nor interrupted the journey for side trips. Eliezer, focused from the beginning on accomplishing his task, faithful to his Master to the last detail,

---

[29] Rebekah's life with Isaac has certain bents in it which do not represent the Bride, so one cannot carry this illustration to certain aspects of Rebekah's life., nor Isaac as the groom, either.

CHAPTER 3
His Bride's Creed

completes the journey, trusting in YeHoVaH, carefully leading the bride along.

PROPHETIC PICTURE EXPLAINED
In summary, the Bride of God, *chosen out of the world from a specified family*[30], initially encounters the Holy Spirit. The Holy Spirit, then, opens the door to her relationship with Her Beloved. With the bridal price given, the Holy Spirit presents the marriage proposal to the Bride. After the Bride *willingly accepts* the proposal, the Holy Spirit lavishes the Bride with wonderful gifts.

Next, He accompanies and safely guides the Bride on her journey to unite with her Betrothed. Without that guidance, the Bride would flounder, not knowing which way to go! Throughout that journey to her destination, the Bride develops a close relationship with the Holy Spirit, the fruit of which produces a single eye, which looks for her Betrothed, *alone*. The Holy Spirit, as seen in the servant of Abraham, additionally cares for the Bride's natural needs such as feeding, protecting, and guiding her on her journey to her Betrothed.

---

[30] Those committed & part of salvation's plan in Messiah.

VALUABLE LESSONS

In this amazing story, we receive wonderful truths.

- Since Rebekah knew not the way to her betrothed's home, the servant lead the way. As Rebekah left her home for her new life and her union with her intended, she committed herself, totally, to the servant's care. Likewise, the Bride of YeHoVaH knows not the way, but recognizing the role of the Holy Spirit, committing herself to His tender love and care.
- Rebekah's kinship with Abraham's family suggests that God's Bride originates from the same lineage and culture as His seed. In other words, the Bride originates from the same seed of holiness, which flows from YeHoVaH. While it is the job of the Holy Spirit, which accompanies the Bride every step of the way, to bring those truths to light, it's the job of the Bride to listen:

Psalm 43:3
   3 O send out thy light and thy truth: let them lead me; let them bring me unto thy holy hill, and to thy tabernacles.

CHAPTER 3
His Bride's Creed

YeHoVaH's Bride accepts the precepts, principles and commands of scripture, yielding to the Holy Spirit's prompting, thus manifesting the fruit of the Spirit. Also, the Bride fulfills God's commands to love Him with all her heart, mind, soul and strength, and to love her neighbour as herself.

This summary of the commandments of YeHoVaH becomes the Bride's Creed! It is hers to learn, understand and obey:

THE BRIDE'S CREED

1. Love the Lord your God
With all your being (heart, mind, soul & strength).

2. Love your neighbour

3. Love yourself

Matthew 22:37-40

HIS BRIDE'S WARFARE

"For the weapons of our warfare [are] not carnal, but mighty through God to the pulling down of strong holds;"

2 Corinthians 10:4

It seems a lovely thought to think that in life, everything we do is well received. Unfortunately, that simply is not so. People, even with the best of intentions, find themselves in a situation where others absolutely disagree with them. Take the situation, recently, as the world engaged in a war against Covid-19.

During this worldwide pandemic, government administrators of every nation poured their efforts, financial and otherwise, to help the population of their nation survive this pandemic. Yet, in every nation, no matter how

CHAPTER 4
His Bride's Warfare

hard they tried, some people objected to their government's tactics. Some objections may be justified; however, the point is that wherever a thing occurs, someone, somewhere, somehow disagrees. Rights to free choice do propagate such responses.

Negative responses also occur when as God's Bride moves forward, fulfilling her mandate. Opposition arises from many different sources. Some of those sources arise from human beings, which may or may not change their mind.

> **However negative their reaction, the Bride's response God already delegated to her:** *respond in love.*

Obviously, then, humankind, no matter the intensity of the objections levied against God's Bride, do not fall within the category of the "enemy". Never! It does the Bride well to remember that there are two major battlefields, which she engages, sometimes furiously:

1) The Battlefield of the Mind
2) The Battlefield of Satanic Forces

THE WARRIOR BRIDE
Advancing God's Kingdom Through Warfare

THE BATTLEFIELD OF THE MIND

As God's Bride moves forward to fulfill her mandate on this earth, keep in mind that her members, *(those representatives of heaven upon this earth)*, live in mortal bodies. Thus, the Word of God admonishes them to look past the surface of the problem which faces them, to examine what exists behind the scenes.

Paul, the Apostle, puts it this way:

> 2 Corinthians 10:1-6
> 1 Now I Paul myself beseech you by the meekness and gentleness of Christ, who in presence [am] base among you, but being absent am bold toward you: 2 But I beseech [you], that I may not be bold when I am present with that confidence, wherewith I think to be bold against some, which think of us as if we walked according to the flesh. 3 For though we walk in the flesh, we do not war after the flesh: 4 (For the weapons of our warfare [are] not carnal, but mighty through God to the pulling down of strong holds;) 5 Casting down imaginations, and every high thing that exalteth itself against the knowledge of God, and bringing into captivity every thought to the obedience of

CHAPTER 4
His Bride's Warfare

Christ; 6 And having in a readiness to revenge all disobedience, when your obedience is fulfilled.

In Paul's opening dialogue, he begs his listeners, by the meekness and gentleness of Messiah, to listen to him. This interesting opening speaks volumes, for the meekness[31] and gentleness of Messiah, form the basis of the Bride moving forward in power and strength!

Following those opening words, Paul, reminds believers that he walked among them humbly, however, when absent, his voice must carry boldness in order for them to hear him. Again, Paul begs them to remember that he does not wish to be bold with them, but unfortunately, he must be that way because of the ones who think that the Apostles, including Paul, walk according to the flesh.

In other words, Paul preferred not to be bold, but rather meek, however, some accused Paul and others of not walking by the Spirit of God. Paul, therefore, addressed them, not allowing his fleshly mind to respond to their accusations,

---

[31] Meek, the English word, originates from a Norse word "mjukr", which means strength under control.

but rather, he responded with the wisdom of God.

Paul reminds his reading audience that indeed, he lives in human form, *in the flesh*. Nevertheless, he will not war with them in a fleshly manner[32]. Paul won't allow *his mind to receive accusations* which might anger him or push him to the point where he would pick up weapons of earth. No, Paul would neither accuse, nor shout, nor call them names, nor use a sword, an arrow or spear. Paul's weapons, the one's of his choice, do not originate from this earth! They are not carnal, fleshly, nor made to damage or wound the flesh, nor any part of it.

Paul's weapons originate in God. With the Word of God, Paul guards his heart and mind. Whenever, he encounters strongholds of the flesh, he pulls them down. Yes, no matter their earthly origin, whether base or high-minded, if it seeks to rise itself above the authority of the Word of God,[33] Paul holds it captive. He, then, pulls it into alignment with the principles of

---

[32] He is not about to engage in a shouting battle, within or without a letter!
[33] The knowledge of God

CHAPTER 4
His Bride's Warfare

God's kingdom, rejecting that which is not godly.

Every thought, no matter its source, members of the Bride must pull into alignment, into obedience with the mandate of Messiah. In other words, those things which object and fight against the truth, Paul sets in the light of the truth. In that way, Paul keeps his thoughts under control so that he is not led of the flesh but rather of the Spirit. When Paul responds, Messiah responds through him. Paul, obviously, guards his heart and mind[34], receiving only that which Messiah verifies. In this manner, Paul possesses a readiness to revenge all disobedience, by fulfilling his obedience to the Torah[35].

Paul, as seen in this section of scripture, keeps his eyes and mind on that awesome Creed of the Bride! He knows that flesh and blood will corrupt. He knows that corruption propagates further problems such as lies, deceptions, delusions and much more, which aim to remove a person from their place of peace in Messiah.

---

[34] Philippians 4:6-8
[35] Torah means instructions of God, here!

Yet therein Paul remains and admonishes members of the Bride to remain also:

Philippians 4:6-8
> 6 Be careful for nothing; but in every thing by prayer and supplication with thanksgiving let your requests be made known unto God. 7 And the peace of God, which passeth all understanding, shall keep your hearts and minds through Christ Jesus. 8 Finally, brethren, whatsoever things are true, whatsoever things [are] honest, whatsoever things [are] just, whatsoever things [are] pure, whatsoever things [are] lovely, whatsoever things [are] of good report; if [there be] any virtue, and if [there be] any praise, think on these things.

BATTLEFIELD OF SATANIC FORCES

Since the Bride of whom we speak, *functions spiritually*, it is *the spiritual opposition* to her multi-faceted operations which warrants the weaponry of the Bride's defense and employment of her weaponry. Thus, Scripture gives many ways in which to overcome and be victorious on that battlefield of man verses the satanic realm. Most of that weaponry follows in

CHAPTER 4
His Bride's Warfare

the subsequent chapters of this book. In this chapter, we'll acknowledge the existence of spiritual entities, what most believers today call satanic forces.

Once again, the Apostle Paul hits the nail on the head as he admonishes members of the Bride to wear their spiritual armour. In doing that, he clearly makes it known that the Bride, whether she likes it or not, has a spiritual enemy. That enemy, which is not part of the flesh and blood realm, is nevertheless real and ready to fight against her with every weapon in its arsenal. Therefore, the Bride wears armour and defends herself:

Ephesians 6:10-20
   10 ¶ Finally, my brethren, be strong in the Lord, and in the power of his might. 11 Put on the whole armour of God, that ye may be able to stand against the wiles of the devil. 12 For we wrestle not against flesh and blood, but against principalities, against powers, against the rulers of the darkness of this world, against spiritual wickedness in high [places]. 13 Wherefore take unto you the whole armour of God, that ye may be able to withstand in the evil

day, and having done all, to stand. 14 Stand therefore, having your loins girt about with truth, and having on the breastplate of righteousness; 15 And your feet shod with the preparation of the gospel of peace; 16 Above all, taking the shield of faith, wherewith ye shall be able to quench all the fiery darts of the wicked.

17 And take the helmet of salvation, and the sword of the Spirit, which is the word of God: 18 Praying always with all prayer and supplication in the Spirit, and watching thereunto with all perseverance and supplication for all saints; 19 ¶ And for me, that utterance may be given unto me, that I may open my mouth boldly, to make known the mystery of the gospel, 20 For which I am an ambassador in bonds: that therein I may speak boldly, as I ought to speak.

Paul's admonition commands a strength in the Lord, so the Bride stands in the power of His might. This is key! No one entity resists the powers of darkness unless they are positioned in God and know how to use His designed weaponry.

CHAPTER 4
His Bride's Warfare

THE WHOLE ARMOUR

As the Bride dons her armour, she prepares[36] to stand against the schemes of the adversary, ha satan[37]. That armour becomes necessary because the warfare is not against human beings (not against flesh and blood as Paul admonished earlier). Rather, Paul defines the spiritual entities which stand against the advancement of the Bride as she seeks to bring the Kingdom of God into the lives of others:

- Principalities
- Powers
- Rulers of the darkness of this world
- Spiritual wickedness in high [places].

These spiritual entities existed in earlier ages, exist now, and will continue to exist as long as this world operates within its present parameters. Paul, speaking for God, wants the Bride overcoming these entities! She cannot fall victim due to her ignorance! No, her destiny cries for victory! Therefore, she must take up the whole armour of God. There is but one reason why this is so! It is to fortify her to stand

---

[36] This is a personal choice and commitment of individual believers.
[37] The devil.

tall in the evil day, the day which presses against her to cause her downfall. She is to hold on to that armour, which a few verses later he describes. This Bride, God formed as victorious! She must stand with:

- HER LOINS wrapped in truth.
- HER BREASTPLATE of righteousness fastened in place.
- HER FEET shoed with the readiness of the gospel of peace.
- HER SHIELD that of faith, ready to extinguish which extinguishes every fiery dart shot at her.
- HER HELMET, which is that of salvation which guards the mind.
- HER SWORD, which is the Word of God, *(which she speaks in season and out of season. That word goes upward to God for promises received, speaks towards man for their liberty, and becomes a powerful weapon against ha satan to cause his forces to cease and desist, to stop their engagement and set captives free.)*[38]
- PRAYING ALWAYS IN THE SPIRIT, *(which means direct, clear and distinct*

---

[38] Author's added comments

CHAPTER 4
His Bride's Warfare

answers from God, which arrive in all circumstances to change those circumstances and bring in those of God's design.)[39]
- WATCHING with all perseverance and supplication for all saints, especially those on the front lines, boldly declaring the gospel of truth. [40]

Thus, you have the Bride prepared to engage in warfare which makes her stronger, but more importantly, sees captives set free.

Here you have the reason for the WARRIOR BRIDE!

In other words, the Bride engages in a spiritual battle, using spiritual weapons to see ha satan defeated and those kept in the claws of death and spiritual bondage, set free! It is not her entire call! It is not her entire mandate; however, the Bride must respond to a wicked and destructive spiritual enemy which seeks to undermine and destroy life, both temporal and eternal.

---

[39] Author's added comments
[40] Incorporates verse 18 to 20.

THE WARRIOR BRIDE
Advancing God's Kingdom Through Warfare

Out of love for her heavenly Bridegroom and for humanity, the Bride wages a spiritual battle, pushing back the enemy so that others may receive the promises of God, enter His Kingdom and live eternally.

In the following section, The Bride Mobilized, we'll define her weapons used to complete this task. In doing so, we'll investigate, thoroughly, the duties of:

THE WARRIOR BRIDE.

SECTION 2

THE BRIDE MOBILIZED

Part 1: To Love Our God

In Part 1, 2 and 3 of section 2, we identify *some of the spiritual weapons of warfare,* which God gave to the Bride to withstand the wiles of ha satan. These weapons of warfare form unique tools that make the Bride successful in her stance against the spiritual forces of darkness. One of the greatest of those weapons, God gave to the Bride all wrapped up in the Bride's Creed, which of course summarizes the Law and the Prophets.

Thus, as we move into this section entitled, The Bride Mobilized, we unwrap some mighty weaponry, all formed around these words:
"Thou shalt love the Lord thy God with all thy heart, and with all thy soul, and with all thy strength, and with all thy mind; and thy neighbour as thyself." Luke 10:27

HIS WEAPONRY OF HIS WORSHIP

"«To the chief Musician, A Song [or] Psalm.» Make a joyful noise unto God, all ye lands: Sing forth the honour of his name: make his praise glorious. Say unto God, How terrible [art thou in] thy works! through the greatness of thy power shall thine enemies submit themselves unto thee. All the earth shall worship thee and shall sing unto thee; they shall sing [to] thy name. Selah.
Psalm 66:1-4

King David, in accordance with the records of Israel's history, stands out as the greatest king who ever ruled Israel. Under King David's leadership, Israel gained and controlled all the territory YeHoVaH

CHAPTER 5
His Weaponry of His Worship

assigned to that nation.[41] No other king of Israel, before or after King David, ever equalled the legacy that King David left behind. His skill as a God-ordained King set Israel in a place of greatness and laid out a magnificent pattern for other generations to follow. Those who utilized King David's same methods, enjoyed enormous victory, both spiritually and physically. Those who did not, saw the nation decline considerably. What was that pattern the Bible tells us that King David set in place as a guide for a successful reign for all future generations?

To answer that question, step back in the Bible to the time when Israel's first king reigned. At his inauguration, King Saul looked promising. His stature, taller than others around him, as well as his moral excellence, seemed to make him a good choice.[42]

---

[41] David had nations subjugated to his kingship, and as was the custom in those days, tribute came to him from those nations.

[42] 1 Samuel 9:2 And he had a son, whose name [was] Saul, a choice young man, and a goodly: and [there was] not among the children of Israel *a **goodlier*** (good moral excellence) person than he: from his shoulders and upward [he was] higher than any of the people.

However, a short time into Saul's reign, King Saul demonstrate that his outward appearance did not represent his true essence. A study of his reign as king from the beginning onwards, demonstrates that Saul valued himself, which included his own ways and judgments, as well as the ways of his people, *above the ways of God*.

In the early events of Saul's reign as king, he allowed the people to take the spoil of the battle, which should have been destroyed.[43] To make matters worse, he allowed them to offer this spoil of battle, that which cost them nothing, as a sacrifice to YeHoVaH. For this, Samuel, the prophet, rebukes Saul:

> 1 Samuel 15:19-23
> 19 Wherefore then didst thou not obey the voice of YeHoVaH, but didst fly upon the spoil, and didst evil in the sight of YeHoVaH? 20 And Saul said unto Samuel, Yea, I have obeyed the voice of YeHoVaH, and have gone the way which YeHoVaH sent me, and have brought Agag the king of Amalek, and have utterly destroyed the Amalekites. 21 But the people took of the

---

[43] 1 Samuel 15:21

CHAPTER 5
His Weaponry of His Worship

spoil, sheep and oxen, the chief of the things which should have been utterly destroyed, to sacrifice unto YeHoVaH thy God in Gilgal. 22 And Samuel said, Hath YeHoVaH [as great] delight in burnt offerings and sacrifices, as in obeying the voice of YeHoVaH? Behold, to obey [is] better than sacrifice, [and] to hearken than the fat of rams. 23 For rebellion [is as] the sin of witchcraft, and stubbornness [is as] iniquity and idolatry. Because thou hast rejected the word of YeHoVaH, he hath also rejected thee from [being] king.

Even though, earlier, the Bible stated Saul possessed good moral excellence above all the children of Israel,[44] when he stepped into the role as king, he elevated his own personal judgments above the commands of God. Throughout his reign, Saul failed to obey God and correctly represent the true King of Israel to Israel, and onlookers as well.[45] Saul, as Israel's first king, with much room to set an example for all kings, instead set a negative example.

---

[44] 1 Samuel 9:2
[45] King David knew YeHoVaH was the true king of Israel, and he, but his representative.

God, however, raised up another person who both obeyed Him and accurately represented the true King of Israel:

1 Samuel 16:13-19

13 Then Samuel took the horn of oil and anointed him in the midst of his brethren: and the Spirit of YeHoVaH came upon David from that day forward. So, Samuel rose up, and went to Ramah. 14 ¶ But the Spirit of YeHoVaH departed from Saul, and an evil spirit from YeHoVaH troubled him. 15 And Saul's servants said unto him, Behold now, an evil spirit from God troubleth thee. 16 Let our lord now command thy servants, [which are] before thee, to seek out a man, [who is] a cunning player on an harp: and it shall come to pass, when the evil spirit from God is upon thee, that he shall play with his hand, and thou shalt be well. 17 And Saul said unto his servants, Provide me now a man that can play well, and bring [him] to me. 18 Then answered one of the servants, and said, Behold, I have seen a son of Jesse the Bethlehemite, [that is] cunning in playing, and a mighty valiant man, and a man of war, and prudent in matters, and a

CHAPTER 5
His Weaponry of His Worship

comely[46] person, and YeHoVaH [is] with him. 19 Wherefore Saul sent messengers unto Jesse, and said, Send me David thy son, which [is] with the sheep.

Here, David enters the scene of Israel's government, not as the anointed King that God made him, but humble as a person who served the present King of Israel. He did so as a young man, who cleverly played his musical instrument, and as a mighty valiant man, a man of war, good looking yet wise in all matters. Above all these attributes, most of which Saul thought important, scripture relates one more thing:

> 1 Samuel 13:14
> "But now thy kingdom shall not continue: YeHoVaH hath sought him a man after his own heart, and YeHoVaH hath commanded him [to be] captain over his people, because thou hast not kept [that] which YeHoVaH commanded thee."

David, with his heart steadily fixed on obeying YeHoVaH, gives us **a major key** to his success

---

[46] Good looking, fair in appearance.

as king. King David honoured and loved YeHoVaH with all his being. David, in doing so, spent his life fulfilling the first commandment of God[47]:

> Deuteronomy 6: 5
> 5 And thou shalt love YeHoVaH thy God with all thine heart, and with all thy soul, and with all thy might.

David, by surrendering his heart to God and loving Him with all his being, tangibly expressed how much he valued God. In other words, David showed God and others the "worth" he put upon YeHoVaH.

David, in valuing YeHoVaH as his greatest treasure, showed YeHoVaH as worth everything!

In doing so, David gave to God His due *worthship*[48], or in today's vernacular, "worship."

---

[47] In looking at King David's life, we see that he also fulfilled the second commandment as well. However, he slipped with Bathsheba. Nevertheless, He repented and still stands as a model king of Israel.

[48] Worthship, a good old English word, became worship centuries ago.

CHAPTER 5
His Weaponry of His Worship

WORSHIP IN DAVID'S REIGN
King David, as a model king of Israel, incorporated additional forms of worship, as well. On Mt. Zion in Jerusalem, David erected a tent and in it rested the Ark of the Covenant, which represents the throne of YeHoVaH. Scripture calls that place of worship the Tabernacle of David.

David, who had a great love for the Word of God, instructed YeHoVaH's priests to study the "Torah", the instructions of God. Through these instructions they would, in turn, teach the people. Additionally, as priests taught, David ordered twenty-four hours, seven days a week praise to YeHoVaH. David, of course, saw to the financial support of these priests so they could spend their time in these all-important tasks.

David understood the importance of honouring God with words, actions and finances; therefore, he employed the thousands of priests ministering before YeHoVaH, as well as erected elaborate banners honouring the presence of the true King of Israel, who dwelt within the Tabernacle on Mt. Zion. Praise songs, trumpets blaring and priests singing to YeHoVaH, constantly and consistently, throughout King David's reign, honoured YeHoVaH's name and proclaimed His greatness. This worship style set a precedence in the reign of King David, *and his legacy* invited other descendants of David to follow suit. Some did. Most did not.

One of the ones who followed suit, however, was Jehoshaphat. Of him, scripture declares:

2 Chronicles 17:3-5

"3 And YeHoVaH was with Jehoshaphat, because he walked in the first ways of his father David and sought not unto Baalim; 4 But sought to the God [YeHoVaH] of his father, and walked in his commandments, and not after the doings of Israel. 5 Therefore YeHoVaH stablished the kingdom in his hand; and all Judah brought to Jehoshaphat presents; and he had riches and honour in abundance."

In this passage, we read that Jehoshaphat walked in the ways of his father, David, which included seeking YeHoVaH and walking in His commandments.

YeHoVaH, in turn, as His Word promises, honoured Jehoshaphat. YeHoVaH established Jehoshaphat's reign, prospered him, and also

CHAPTER 5
His Weaponry of His Worship

protected him from his enemies and their attacks upon him. One such attack came during his reign, when the Moabites and Ammonites decided to dethrone Jehoshaphat and take Jerusalem[49] for themselves. Thus, as a great multitude they came against Jehoshaphat to take the kingdom. When Jehoshaphat heard of their plot, he proclaimed a fast and sought YeHoVaH. Then, they gathered together to hear the counsel of the Almighty:

> 2 Chronicles 20:14-17
> 14 Then upon Jahaziel the son of Zechariah, the son of Benaiah, the son of Jeiel, the son of Mattaniah, a Levite of the sons of Asaph, came the Spirit of YeHoVaH in the midst of the congregation; 15 And he said, Hearken ye, all Judah, and ye inhabitants of Jerusalem, and thou king Jehoshaphat, Thus saith YeHoVaH unto you, Be not afraid nor dismayed by reason of this great multitude; for the battle [is] not yours, but God's. 16 To morrow go ye down against

---

[49] Jerusalem lay in a very strategic place for gaining wealth. Own Jerusalem and you had great possibilities of economic wealth. Not to mention the fact that Jerusalem sat in higher country, which position made it extremely advantageous during times of war.

them: behold, they come up by the cliff of Ziz; and ye shall find them at the end of the brook, before the wilderness of Jeruel. 17 Ye shall not [need] to fight in this [battle]: set yourselves, stand ye [still], and see the salvation of YeHoVaH with you, O Judah and Jerusalem: fear not, nor be dismayed; to morrow go out against them: for YeHoVaH [will be] with you.

This prophet of God, Jahaziel, declared a true word from YeHoVaH, which promised total deliverance to Israel. Furthermore, he acknowledged that YeHoVaH saw, *this battle to remove Jehoshaphat and all Israel from the land,* as His Battle!

Jehoshaphat believed the prophet and set out to battle, employing a strange tactic: *singing praises*[50] *to YeHoVaH, with the worshippers in front of the army!*[51]

---

[50] This collection of priests with the singers, instruments and the like already operated in Jerusalem under Jehoshaphat's reign. They simply moved in the worship manner they used!

[51] Normal war tactics would send fighting men to the front to show the enemy a strong resistant force. Jehoshaphat believed the Word of God and praised Him for fighting the battle for Israel!

CHAPTER 5
His Weaponry of His Worship

2 Chronicles 20:18-21

> 18 And Jehoshaphat bowed his head with [his] face to the ground: and all Judah and the inhabitants of Jerusalem fell before YeHoVaH, worshipping YeHoVaH. 19 And the Levites, of the children of the Kohathites, and of the children of the Korhites, stood up to praise YeHoVaH God of Israel with a loud voice on high. 20 ¶ And they rose early in the morning and went forth into the wilderness of Tekoa: and as they went forth, Jehoshaphat stood and said, Hear me, O Judah, and ye inhabitants of Jerusalem; Believe in YeHoVaH your God, so shall ye be established; believe his prophets, so shall ye prosper. 21 And when he had consulted with the people, he appointed singers unto YeHoVaH, and that should praise the beauty of holiness, as they went out before the army, and to say, Praise YeHoVaH; for his mercy [endureth] for ever

Jehoshaphat appointed singers unto YeHoVaH, to go out before the army! Their message, or their weapon of warfare, "Praise YeHoVaH! For His mercy endures forever!" YeHoVaH honoured their faith, trust and worship:

THE WARRIOR BRIDE
Advancing God's Kingdom Through Warfare

2 Chronicles 20:22-26

22 And when they began to sing and to praise, YeHoVaH set ambushments against the children of Ammon, Moab, and mount Seir, which were come against Judah; and they were smitten. 23 For the children of Ammon and Moab stood up against the inhabitants of mount Seir, utterly to slay and destroy [them]: and when they had made an end of the inhabitants of Seir, everyone helped to destroy another. 24 And when Judah came toward the watch tower in the wilderness, they looked unto the multitude, and behold, they [were] dead bodies fallen to the earth, and none escaped.

25 And when Jehoshaphat and his people came to take away the spoil of them, they found among them in abundance both riches with the dead bodies, and precious jewels, which they stripped off for themselves, more than they could carry away: and they were three days in gathering of the spoil, it was so much. 26 And on the fourth day they assembled themselves in the valley of Berachah; for there they blessed YeHoVaH: therefore, the

CHAPTER 5
His Weaponry of His Worship

name of the same place was called, The valley of Berachah, unto this day.

Jehoshaphat knew, as did the people with him, the benefit of worship. Their praises became their strategy, their weapon. Their worship to YeHoVaH and their faith in Him and His promises became their defense against a wicked foe. Why? Because this battle, by which their enemy sought their total annihilation, belonged to YeHoVaH.

HIS WEAPONRY OF WORSHIP
King David and Jehoshaphat gave God the worship due Him, namely, to love Him with their heart, mind, soul and strength. Such devotion produced obedience to the commandments and precepts of the Almighty. In addition, their lifestyle lays out a powerful weapon of warfare, a pattern for success, which every generation should employ.

Likewise, in every generation, the Bride of YeHoVaH[52] does well to wield this same weaponry! First, by loving God with every part of their being, and serving Him by obeying His

---

[52] Yeshua (same Bride)

commandments and precepts, learning His ways, and functioning in them. Next, by pouring every aspect of their being into His service, including the finances, time, and energies given for that purpose. In that way, the Bride employs tactics which contribute to her success in expanding the Kingdom of God. Such behaviour truly defeats the Bride's greatest enemy, ha satan, (the adversary), the accuser.

Additionally, as the Bride, propelled by heart worship, moves into verbal worship, she expresses that love vocally, in an audible way. As the Bride models the elaborate worship shown in the Tabernacle of David,[53] she draws others to recognize YeHoVaH's greatness, and thus opens a door for others to know Him. YeHoVaH's arm of deliverance goes with the Warrior Bride as she reaches out to bring to YeHoVaH the most precious commodity upon the earth: *souls*. Indeed, as the Bride moves ahead in this manner, God moves forward, too, touching those troubled souls who wish to know Him and serve Him.

---

[53] That worship incorporated banners, trumpets, tambourines, prophetic voices singing unto YeHoVaH, and continual sacrifices of praise.

CHAPTER 5
His Weaponry of His Worship

Furthermore, such honouring of YeHoVaH draws heaven into action to fight for humankind's spiritual freedom and eternal destiny! Such weaponry, with all its multifaceted aspects of worship, from personal commitment to service and onward, delights YeHoVaH, and at the same time, robs the enemy of his goods: *those precious souls which God so longs to see set free!* This aspect of worship, which proves to be an important secret weapon, the Warrior Bride cannot afford to overlook!

Remember, the Warrior Bride, whose very image in armour might cause some to struggle, aims her sights at removing that which seeks to kill, rob or destroy. Weapons of the Warrior Bride, which raises the heart, voice and eyes to the Almighty God of Israel, seeks the One Who is able to save, heal and deliver! It is with this heart that the Warrior Bride seeks God above all things. This aspect of warfare focuses on the One Who alone can change hearts! How beautiful is that aspect of the Warrior Bride!

Psalm 3:4-8
  4 ¶ I cried unto YeHoVaH with my voice, and he heard me out of his holy hill. Selah.

THE WARRIOR BRIDE
Advancing God's Kingdom Through Warfare

5 I laid me down and slept; I awaked; for YeHoVaH sustained me. 6 I will not be afraid of ten thousand of people, that have set [themselves] against me round about.
7 Arise, O YeHoVaH; save me, O my God: for thou hast smitten all mine enemies [upon] the cheek bone; thou hast broken the teeth of the ungodly. 8 Salvation [belongeth] unto YeHoVaH: thy blessing [is] upon thy people. Selah.

HIS WEAPONRY OF HIS NAME

Sing unto YeHoVaH, all the earth; shew forth from day to day his salvation. Declare his glory among the heathen, his marvellous works among all nations. For great [is] YeHoVaH, and greatly to be praised: he also [is] to be feared above all gods. For all the gods of the people [are] idols: but YeHoVaH made the heavens. Glory and honour [are] in his presence; strength and gladness [are] in his place. Give unto the YeHoVaH, ye kindreds of the people, give unto YeHoVaH glory and strength.

Give unto YeHoVaH the glory [due] unto his name: *bring an offering and come before him: worship YeHoVaH in the beauty of holiness.*

1 Chronicles 16:23-29

Honour in today's world, holds a slightly different meaning than in ancient times. In the days when the

CHAPTER 6
His Weaponry of His Name

author penned the above scripture, man paid great honour to rulers such as kings, or to those who led exemplary lives such as heroes of war. To some, in those days, to have a name worthy of honour and respect meant more than to possess a treasure house full of goods. We hear that clearly stated in the Book of Proverbs:

> Proverbs 22:1
> 1 A [good] name [is] rather to be chosen than great riches, [and] loving favour rather than silver and gold.
>
> Ecclesiastes 7:1
> 1 A good name [is] better than precious ointment; and the day of death than the day of one's birth.

Today, professional companies do their best to develop commercial branding, with the idea of promoting their special product. They name the product with something easy to remember, and then boost that name by bombarding the market with many aspects of advertising. They may even enlist important people, such as famous athletes or actors to endorse their product. Some accept and endorse the product, whether or not they ever used it! [54] All that has one purpose: *to increase income.* Such use of honouring names, in comparison to the value of a name in Bible days, seems somewhat superficial. In those days, a name meant everything!

While, today, most people desire to have a good reputation attached to their name, in comparison to ancient times, the honour given to names measures considerably less, *especially when it comes to honouring the name of God.*

Besides the obvious reason of not using the name of God in vain, respect has lessened for the name of God in many ways, simply because conspirators schemed to hide it. Hiding that name did great dishonour to the Loving, Living God Who releases great benefits for those who actually use His Name! [55] Silencers of the name of YeHoVaH, for example, demanded that, out of respect God's Name be declared too holy to pronounce. Thus, believers, over the centuries, found themselves saying, "the Lord", rather

---

[54] Some nations now have laws to prevent a person endorsing a product they never used.
[55] A presentation of those benefits follows.

CHAPTER 6
His Weaponry of His Name

than using God's name. This practice, which in its origin claimed to save lives, instead, did the reverse! How can one call upon the Name of God to be saved, if they know not the Name?

> Romans 10:14
> 14 How then shall they call on him in whom they have not believed? and how shall they believe in him of whom they have not heard? and how shall they hear without a preacher?

Without understanding the consequences nor the dynamics of not using God's name, believers became partners to a secret conspiracy to hide the name of the Living God. [56] Truly, that does great dishonour to God. That action stands in direct opposition to commands of God, as seen in the Word.[57] Obedient believers, as the Word commands, honoured God by speaking His Name. They honoured Him as they declared His Name and His Works!

In the book of Psalms, over 700 times, the Psalmists refers to the Name of God, using it

---

[56] For information in that regard, see the appendix.
[57] That point proves itself true in the scriptures on the following pages.

often. Clearly, these authors never substituted that precious name with the title, Lord, but left it fully written out for future generations to declare. These Psalmists spoke the Name, knowing full well the benefit of its use.

On the next few pages, scriptures from the Psalms invite readers to see some of the benefits of speaking God's Name and gives opportunity to shed manmade traditions contrary to the Word. These few scriptures, remember, give *only a few highlights of the use of God's Name*, nevertheless, they show that the use of God's Name employs a powerful weapon, and brings a formidable impact.[58]

FULFILL A COMMAND
Psalm 68:4

4 Sing unto God, sing praises to his name: extol him that rideth upon the heavens by his name JAH, and rejoice before him.

Psalm 113:1

1 Praise ye YeHoVaH. Praise, O ye servants of YeHoVaH, praise the name of YeHoVaH.

---

[58] No wonder our adversary wants it left unspoken!

CHAPTER 6
His Weaponry of His Name

Psalm 74:21
> 21 O let not the oppressed return ashamed: let the poor and needy praise thy name.

DEFEAT THE ENEMY

Psalm 5:11
> 11 But let all those that put their trust in thee rejoice: let them ever shout for joy, because thou defendest them: let them also that love thy name be joyful in thee.

Psalm 9:10
> 10 And they that know thy name will put their trust in thee: for thou, YeHoVaH, hast not forsaken them that seek thee.

Psalm 20:1
> 1 YeHoVaH hear thee in the day of trouble; the name of the God of Jacob defend thee;

Psalm 44:5
> 5 Through thee will we push down our enemies: through thy name will we tread them under that rise up against us.

EXPERIENCE AMAZING THINGS

Psalm 75:1
> 1 Unto thee, O God, do we give thanks, *unto thee* do we give thanks: for *that thy name is near* thy wondrous works declare.

Psalm 79:9
> 9 Help us, O God of our salvation, for the glory of thy name: and deliver us, and *purge away our sins*, for thy name's sake.

Psalm 83:18
> 18 That *men may know* that thou, whose name alone *is* JEHOVAH[59], art the most high over all the earth.

Psalm 91:14
> 14 Because he hath set his love upon me, therefore *will I deliver him: I will set him on high*, because he hath known my name

Psalm 106:8
> 8 Nevertheless he saved them for his name's sake, that he might make his mighty power to be known.

RECEIVE BLESSING AND BENEFITS
Psalm 118:10
> 10 All nations compassed me about: but in the name of YeHoVaH will I destroy them.

---

[59] Way KJV wrote it in their text for this verse.

CHAPTER 6
His Weaponry of His Name

Psalm 119:55
> 55 I have remembered thy name, O YeHoVaH, in the night, and have kept thy law.

Psalm 124:8
> 8 Our help *is* in the name of YeHoVaH, who made heaven and earth.

Psalm 135:13
> 13 Thy name, YeHoVaH, *endureth* for ever; *and* thy memorial, O YeHoVaH, throughout all generations.

In these few verses, just a small pick of what's available for us within the Psalms, the importance of using the name of God stands out, incredibly! [60]

Using that Great Name brings benefits, while refusal to use it creates many problems such as robbing people of God's help!

By calling upon His Name, He saves us:

---

[60] Why not do a personal study on your own of the benefits of using the Name of God.

SAVED WHEN ATTACKED

Numbers 10:9

9 And if ye go to war in your land against the enemy that oppresseth you, then ye shall blow an alarm with the trumpets; and ye shall be remembered before YeHoVaH your God, and ye shall be saved from your enemies.

SAVED BY DIVINE FAVOUR

Psalm 80:3

3 Turn us again, O God, and cause thy face to shine; and we shall be saved.

Psalm 80:7

7 Turn us again, O God of hosts, and cause thy face to shine; and we shall be saved.

Psalm 80:19

19 Turn us again, O YEHOVAH God of hosts, cause thy face to shine; and we shall be saved.

SAVED FROM SIN

Jeremiah 17:14

14 Heal me, O YEHOVAH, and I shall be healed; save me, and I shall be saved: for thou [art] my praise.

CHAPTER 6
His Weaponry of His Name

Proverbs 28:18
> 18 Whoso walketh uprightly shall be saved: but [he that is] perverse [in his] ways shall fall at once.

Isaiah 45:17
> 17 [But] Israel shall be saved in YeHoVaH with an everlasting salvation: ye shall not be ashamed nor confounded world without end.

Mark 16:16
> 16 He that believeth and is baptized shall be saved; but he that believeth not shall be damned.

John 10:9
> 9 I am the door: by me if any man enter in, he shall be saved, and shall go in and out, and find pasture.

So many great promises rest in calling upon His Name, too many to overlook. In addition, once people know YeHoVaH's Name and call upon it, a place of refuge opens to us, as declared in the scriptures on the following pages:

Psalm 61:3
> 3 For thou hast been a shelter for me, [and] a strong tower from the enemy.

Proverbs 18:10
> 10 The name of YeHoVaH [is] a strong tower: the righteous runneth into it and is safe.

Psalm 61 declares YeHoVaH as a shelter, however, the author of Proverbs goes even further declaring that YeHoVaH's name is a strong tower. This speaks of safety and protection. Similarly, Proverbs 18:10 identifies the Name of YeHoVaH as a strong tower, to which the righteous enter and find safety. YeHoVaH's name falls out of the category of *just any name*. His name contains power and ability to realign the earth with heaven.

Reiterating an earlier comment, no wonder *the spiritual source* behind hiding YeHoVaH's name *(ha satan)*[61] did so! Surely, that enemy (ha satan) who brought such horrible dishonour to the name of YeHoVaH by disallowing its use, needs a complete overthrow to end his plots and

---
[61] Ha satan, the adversary, the accuser, the devil.

CHAPTER 6
His Weaponry of His Name

schemes. With this revealed knowledge of his deeds, his overthrow becomes possible as believers align with the Word and the truth about God's Name.

HIS WEAPONRY OF HIS NAME

People who make up the Warrior Bride, indeed, should know the name of the Living God to Whom they serve, and then, pronounce it and proclaim it. In this way, the travesty, which ha satan set to hide the enormous benefits of using God's Name, falls short of its goal. Those who desperately need these benefits in YeHoVaH's name hear about them, employ them and then rejoice!

Surely, out of love for humankind upon this earth and her Betrothed, the Warrior Bride loving speaks the amazing truth of God's Name. That Name she speaks, to Honour Her Betrothed, understanding this powerful weapon from Heaven's weaponry changes things. Thus, she hides not His Identity nor the power in His Name. As she articulates the mighty Name of YeHoVaH, and of His only begotten Son, Yeshua, she proclaims weapons of honour to benefit all!

THE WARRIOR BRIDE
Advancing God's Kingdom Through Warfare

Surely the righteous shall give thanks unto thy name, YeHoVaH: the upright shall dwell in thy presence.

Psalm 140:13

7

HIS WEAPONRY OF HIS WORD

"For ever, O YEHOVAH, thy word is settled in heaven."

Psalm 119:89

Genesis, the first book within the Canon of Scripture, speaks about the power of the Word of God, for this is how God created the world! With His Word going forth, its resident power within, divided in magnificent ways to form creation:

God's Word divided light from darkness:

Genesis 1:3-5

> 3 ¶ And God said, Let there be light: and there was light. 4 And God saw the light, that [it was] good: and God divided the light from the darkness. 5 And God called the light Day, and the darkness he called Night. And the evening and the morning were the first day.

CHAPTER 7
His Weaponry of His Word

God's Word divided heaven above from heaven below:

Genesis 1:6-8

> 6 ¶ And God said, Let there be a firmament in the midst of the waters, and let it divide the waters from the waters. 7 And God made the firmament and divided the waters which [were] under the firmament from the waters which [were] above the firmament: and it was so. 8 And God called the firmament Heaven. And the evening and the morning were the second day.

God's Word divided land from sea:

Genesis 1:9-10

> 9 ¶ And God said, Let the waters under the heaven be gathered together unto one place, and let the dry [land] appear: and it was so. 10 And God called the dry [land] Earth; and the gathering together of the waters called he Seas: and God saw that [it was] good.

As if these passages did not give enough evidence of God's Word as distinguished above other words, Psalm 29 outlines more dividing properties:

THE WARRIOR BRIDE
Advancing God's Kingdom Through Warfare

**God's Word breaks cedars,
divides flames of fires,
shakes the wilderness:**

Psalm 29:5-8
> 5 The voice of YeHoVaH breaketh the cedars; yea, YeHoVaH breaketh the cedars of Lebanon. 6 He maketh them also to skip like a calf; Lebanon and Sirion like a young unicorn. 7 The voice of YeHoVaH divideth the flames of fire. 8 The voice of YeHoVaH shaketh the wilderness; YeHoVaH shaketh the wilderness of Kadesh.

Keeping this property of God in mind, Apostolic Scriptures carry on the same theme:

Hebrews 4:12
> 12 For the word of God [is] quick, and powerful, and sharper than any two-edged sword, piercing even to the dividing asunder of soul and spirit, and of the joints and marrow, and [is] a discerner of the thoughts and intents of the heart.

God's Word is quick, meaning alive! His Word has life and power! That same Word impacts those who listen. It has a sharpness, unlike

CHAPTER 7
His Weaponry of His Word

other words, and that sharpness pierces deep, splitting apart the very soul from the spirit of a person. That is an intricate cut, for the soul and the spirit so often act as one. Truly, it is humanly impossible to discern the difference, to the human mind, but not for God's Word.

Speaking of the dividing power of God's Word, when it reaches into the depths of man, it does what medical science finds hard to divide, namely, joint and marrow. Indeed, the Word of God exposes the secret things which hide in the depths of a human being. Cutting deep, the Word of God separates the thoughts and intents of that person, showing the true motive.

These motives of the heart, in fact, move the person to make their decisions, good or bad. How awesome a Word of God, Whose very impact contains power to separate the intimate thoughts by which man thinks and decides. Surely, God's Word is no ordinary word!

This theme of dividing, the Apostle Paul carries forth as he admonishes ardent followers of the Way to study the Word of God:

2 Timothy 2:15
> 15 Study to shew thyself approved unto God, a workman that needeth not to be ashamed, rightly dividing the word of truth.

Here we read that a good student of the Word of God rightly divides the Word of truth! To do so means effective learning about God, His Word, His Power and what He desires for us. It also helps as believers follow the encouragement to study God's Word, to remember why God gave it to man in the first place!

A QUICK LOOK AT GOD'S WORD

Sandwiched between two hard covers, we easily hold a modern Bible. For Christians, that Bible contains two sections, one labelled, The Old Covenant, and the other labelled, The New Covenant. This selection and the order in which it came to us, reflects the thoughts of religious leaders over the centuries.

On the other hand, the Jewish Bible holds only one section, which is a record of the First Covenant given to Israel. This Bible, the Tanakh contains three main sections. Its divisions outline a basis for a unique understanding of

CHAPTER 7
His Weaponry of His Word

the Word of God, and its purpose for our lives. Most Christians, unless schooled in Hebrew, do not read this version of the Bible. Perhaps in time, this might change, for the original Hebrew scriptures set within its Hebraic culture, offer great promise to unlock some amazing truths, which years of Christianity, unfortunately, either misunderstood or overlooked.

As we think, further, on God's Word as part of our armour, it seems rather appropriate to take, at least a sneak peek, at the structure of the Tanakh. Who knows, the overview might intrigue many to delve in deeper!

THE TORAH
Moses, the mighty deliverer of Egypt who God called to lead the children of Israel out of slavery, penned this book. While we have an historical account of creation as well as the events before and after the Exodus, it relates additional information. Within its five books, God gave instructions through Moses, to show humankind how to serve Him, how to treat others, and basically, how to live in this world in which He placed us. In other words, if we wish to know the requirements of God for living, refer to the Torah. It instructs us!

THE WORD OF GOD (Tanuk)	
TORAH (Pentateuch) Genesis, Exodus, Leviticus, Numbers, Deuteronomy	This includes the first five books of Moses. It contains God's instructions to mankind on how to worship and serve Him, and how to treat others.
NEV'IM (Prophets) Joshua, Judges; 1 & 2 Samuel, 1 & 2 Kings; Isaiah, Jeremiah, Ezekiel, Hosea, Joel, Amos, Obadiah, Jonah, Micah, Nahum, Habakkuk, Zephaniah, Haggai, Zechariah, Malachi	This includes the voice of YeHoVaH as He spoke through the Prophets calling the People to return to God.
KETUVIM (Writings) Psalms, Proverbs, Job, Song of Songs; Ruth, Lamentations, Ecclesiastes, Esther, Daniel, Ezra, Nehemiah; 1 &2 Chronicles	This includes a record or history of how God kept His promises of both restoration and judgment

CHAPTER 7

His Weaponry of His Word

THE NEV'IM
YeHoVaH raised up prophets to speak to His people. Their main task, as God outlined it, relates God's view on how His People live out the Torah. Prophets call God's people *back to God, engaging them in the idea of heartfelt repentance*. If listeners do repent, God promises certain good things, and if they do not repent, He promises certain unwelcoming things to get their attention and hopefully, turn them around. Within the element of promised things coming, we often see the message of future events prophesied.

However, the Nev'im serves primarily as a mirror to reflect the heart of God as He moved towards His People inviting them to enjoy life, *now and in eternity*. Thus, the Nev'im declares the good paths to walk upon. Thus, it helps to align God's people with God, His commandments, precepts and statutes.

Those who stray from the good path hear what happened in former days, and then, measuring the reality of past history, weigh things out. Hopefully, the study of the Nev'im sees its fruit manifest in true repentance and a complete return to God.

THE KETUVIM

This section contains the writings of those God divinely called to pen *the historical account* of Israel. This section, like the Nev'im, contains prophetic insights, however, ***its main point*** is to record historical events showing Israel's activities and how God kept His Word.

In looking at the Tanakh, understanding the reason for each section, we have an even more accurate measurement to rightly divide the Word of God. In other words, we go back to the very basics of the PURPOSE of each book written, and then, we better understand the aim of the book. For example, we see the book of Ruth. It is found in the historical records, showing the lineage of King David. Without that lineage, proving Yeshua's root as the rightful King of Israel doesn't happen.

Esther, also, shows an important historical fact, and that is how God saved all Israel, through the life of a former orphan girl, who, through the hand of the Almighty God of Israel, married a King. Her intercession on behalf of Israel saved Israel from annihilation. Additionally, it gives hope to every Jewish and Christian believer on the ability of God to deliver in

CHAPTER 7
His Weaponry of His Word

extreme circumstances. It shows God's Sovereignty!

Furthermore, as Christian believers, we have books written to us by Hebrew thinking, God ordained men of the Word, thoroughly grounded in the Torah, Nev'im and Ketuvim. The more we understand the Hebraic scriptures, the more common ground we have to grasp the teachings of the fathers of our faith. As we look at the Word of God, as we embrace it, drawing it close to our hearts, we allow the Holy Spirit to divide and separate our deepest thoughts. We look in the "mirror" of the Word, as James calls it, to see and remember:

James 1:19-25
19 ¶ Wherefore, my beloved brethren, let every man be swift to hear, slow to speak, slow to wrath: 20 For the wrath of man worketh not the righteousness of God.

21 Wherefore lay apart all filthiness and superfluity of naughtiness, and receive with meekness the engrafted word, which is able to save your souls. 22 But be ye doers of the word, and not hearers only, deceiving your own selves. 23 For if any be

a hearer of the word, and not a doer, he is like unto a man beholding his natural face in a glass: 24 For he beholdeth himself, and goeth his way, and straightway forgetteth what manner of man he was. 25 But whoso looketh into the perfect law of liberty, and continueth [therein], he being not a forgetful hearer, but a doer of the work, this man shall be blessed in his deed.

HIS WEAPONRY OF HIS WORD

Realizing such amazing properties as contained within the Word of God, we recognize God's Word as both offensive and defensive, depending upon the circumstances. It becomes offensive in the sense that is cuts or divides as it presents God's viewpoint on matters, such as a call to repentance. At the same time, it becomes defensive as it speaks life to all who hear it, even when it addresses sin issues. Indeed, this is one weapon the Bride must learn to wield well, first, on her own behalf, and then, on behalf of others.

Additionally, the Word of God, whose properties make it comparable to a double-edged sword, cuts deep enough to wound the greatest adversary. Here is where the rubber meets the road: *the defeat of man's greatest*

CHAPTER 7
His Weaponry of His Word

adversary came through the power of the Living God in the life, death and resurrection of His incarnate Son, **Yeshua**.

John 1: 11-14
> 11 He came unto his own, and his own received him not. 12 But as many as received him, to them gave he power to become the sons of God, [even] to them that believe on his name: 13 Which were born, not of blood, nor of the will of the flesh, nor of the will of man, but of God. 14 And the Word was made flesh, and dwelt among us, (and we beheld his glory, the glory as of the only begotten of the Father,) full of grace and truth.

As the Living, incarnate Word of God, Yeshua impacted this world, in ways from which she'll never recover! Through His death, burial, resurrection and ascension to sit at God's right hand, Yeshua wounded the adversary of humankind!

Luke 10:18
> "And he said unto them, I beheld Satan as lightning fall from heaven."

THE WARRIOR BRIDE
Advancing God's Kingdom Through Warfare

For the accomplishment of defeating ha satan, and for all His great accomplishments, which included shedding His own blood on behalf of all humankind, He received a name above all names. Additionally, He received the right to wield all authority in heaven and in earth.

> Matthew 28:18-20
> 18 And Jesus came and spake unto them, saying, All power is given unto me in heaven and in earth. 19 Go ye therefore, and teach all nations, baptizing them in the name of the Father, and of the Son, and of the Holy Ghost: 20 Teaching them to observe all things whatsoever I have commanded you: and, lo, I am with you alway, [even] unto the end of the world. Amen.

Yeshua, with His accomplishments, followed by His lavish gifts, made it possible for the Bride to wield the weaponry of heaven, and thus greatly change the world. Using God's Word as the sword He designed, works wonders as the Warrior Bride speaks out a powerful message to earth's recipients, and gives the Sword also, to spiritual adversaries. The weaponry of His Word, when wielded, moves earth and heaven!

HIS WEAPONRY OF HIS ONENESS

"And they twain shall be one flesh: so, then they are no more twain, but one flesh. 9 What therefore God hath joined together, let not man put asunder. 10 And in the house his disciples asked him again of the same [matter]."

Mark 10:8-10

Yeshua, when asked about divorce, spoke of the unity or oneness which God placed within the marriage. That unity began at the betrothal. To the Jewish mind in ancient Bible days, after the betrothal ceremony took place, the couple, although not united in a sexual union, in the eyes of the Law of Israel, people and God saw the couple as married, as one entity. The physical joining, which came later, solidified the marriage, nevertheless, from

CHAPTER 8
His Weaponry of His Oneness

the day of their betrothal, neither the future bride nor groom had legal permission to look for another mate. Such action they considered adultery. From the first day of the couple's betrothal, their betrothal contract firmly secured their marriage and only a legal divorce could separate them.

Understanding the oneness, that commenced at betrothal in ancient times, helps to make some sense out of the oneness God designed within the relationship of His Bride. As this Bride functions on earth, her oneness with her Betrothed never changes, generation after generation. With the covenant sealed at Mount Sinai, [62]beginning the day of betrothal until Yeshua returns and sets up God's Kingdom upon the earth, this oneness remains a key factor in fulfilling her role.

FIRST COVENANT ONENESS
As already discussed, Israel, as a nation betrothed to YeHoVaH, began on Mt. Sinai. Here, the twelve tribes, as well as her priests serving YeHoVaH, encamped around the Tabernacle of Moses built to house the Ark of

---

[62] Explained in Chapter 2, His Bride Defined.

the Covenant, which represented the throne of the Almighty. This layout pictured a oneness[63] of Israel as a redeemed people, embraced by the Living God, Who created all heaven and earth.

Additionally, Israel, in this early stage, represented God's Kingdom upon the earth. With the Ark of the Covenant as the central theme of life within the entire nation of Israel, they demonstrated the centrality of their oneness with the One Who led them out of Egypt. Whenever they broke camp going to another place, they represented that Kingdom advancing. As they carried the Ark of the Covenant, the throne of YeHoVaH upon the shoulders of the priests, Israel demonstrated the government of God moving with them over the face of the earth.

Israel, as well as all of the nations in the world, whether or not they acknowledge YeHoVaH, He requires them to give an account of their behaviour, corporately and individually. This account holds them responsible to Him for how they live their lives. It includes their response

---

[63] If you are not familiar with this layout, please do some research to ensure you understand it.

CHAPTER 8
His Weaponry of His Oneness

to Him, as well as to humankind. Therefore, God set Israel as a solitaire in a diamond, or more biblically stated, as a light to all nations.[64] Those who desired to be like her could learn to do so. Those who refused, especially those who directly opposed any form of repentance and change, God does judge.

Pictorially, then, as Israel moved forward on her journey, she showed YeHoVaH's Kingdom and His government coming upon the earth. Whenever nations rose up against Israel, such as the Amalekites in Exodus 17, God stood on the side of Israel to show His alignment with them and to see His government established. The throne of YeHoVaH, pictured in the Ark of the Covenant borne along, showed God examining the basis of the encounters with those who strongly opposed Israel. In other words, YeHoVaH judged those nations.

When Israel fought, as in Exodus 17, she did so following YeHoVaH's instructions through Moses. God's hand of Judgment, via His designated kingdom of chosen people, (Israel) became the hand of God's judgment. One thing

---
[64] The Gentiles

becomes clear in that battle in Exodus 17: *YeHoVaH miraculously defended Israel*. While Israel entered that war against those that wanted her destruction, additionally, she walked out the judgment of YeHoVaH, Who actually worked in the background.

Prophetically speaking, Israel, as a representative of the Kingdom of God upon the earth, moved in a oneness with YeHoVaH. As long as their leader carefully followed YeHoVaH's heavenly decisions and counsels, they clearly presented the picture of God moving in their midst. Later, as Israel's history showed, the Bride stepped out of oneness with YeHoVaH, walked away from His laws, precepts and counsels and walked in their own ways. As Israel, therefore, forsook and abandoned the oneness with YeHoVaH, moving forward without Him and His permission, inevitably, in those seasons, Israel walked in defeat. So, this picture of oneness with YeHoVaH, the Bride, moving in conjunction with His instructions and counsel, becomes paramount in representing the

CHAPTER 8
His Weaponry of His Oneness

Kingdom of God and His government to the world. [65]

NEW COVENANT ONENESS
After the cross, representation of the Bride as seen through Israel's outward display, shifted from the Tabernacle and the Ark of the Covenant, (God's Throne) to *an inner* representation:

> 1 Corinthians 12:13
> 13 For by one Spirit are we all baptized into one body, whether [we be] Jews or Gentiles, whether [we be] bond or free; and have been all made to drink into one Spirit.

Through the power of the Holy Spirit, believers walk in a oneness with the Betrothed of Heaven. That oneness, designed by God to shape, direct and move the Bride forward, still represents the Kingdom of God, yet the world does not see its

---

[65] This holds true for Israel, today. As she walks in her role as a light to all nations, arising to a world power within the Middle East, she must remember to maintain her oneness with YeHoVaH. As she walks in that oneness, following God's Laws, commandments and counsels, God *can still use Israel* to demonstrate His Kingdom, His government and His judgments.

complete impact moving in only one area, but one nation. Instead, the Holy Spirit, living and moving within the Betrothed, makes a shift from the outer appearance to a supernatural appearance possible, yet in significant portions throughout the world. Not one nation, also, represents YeHoVaH, but multitudes of nations in Messiah, have a marvellous potential to represent Him *everywhere*. This great shift happened *from* a greater victory, *(that of the cross), for* a greater victory!

Due to the Spirit of God's main function, His unbroken unity with the Godhead, the Betrothed now has potential to function with a greater power and greater influence upon the earth. Similarly, to Israel representing God's Kingdom and Government, the Bride's call comes from heaven to impact the earth with the gospel.

If the Bride clings to the instructions, ways and counsel as guided by the Holy Spirit, she moves in oneness with her Betrothed, and thus advances the Kingdom of God. Her goal, without wavering, must be redemption of souls. Her judgments, those uttered from the throne

CHAPTER 8
His Weaponry of His Oneness

room of Heaven[66], aim at the unseen spiritual world. Her decisions, which model heaven's, function as commands to dethrone the wicked forces of darkness who enslave souls.

Additionally, the Bride offers hope to those caught in the prison houses of ha satan, giving them a way of escape. Such instructions Yeshua received from His Father and thus, the Bride must follow:

> Luke 4:18-19
> "18 The Spirit of YeHoVaH [is] upon me, because he hath anointed me to preach the gospel to the poor; he hath sent me to heal the brokenhearted, to preach deliverance to the captives, and recovering of sight to the blind, to set at liberty them that are bruised, 19 To preach the acceptable year of YeHoVaH."

To those ends, Yeshua came and to those ends, the Bride must follow. This we hear in from the messages found in the Bible, among them this passage from the book of Isaiah:

---

[66] Not the throne of earth as seen in the First Covenant!

THE WARRIOR BRIDE
Advancing God's Kingdom Through Warfare

Isaiah 11:1-5

> 1 ¶ And there shall come forth a rod out of the stem of Jesse, and a Branch shall grow out of his roots: 2 And the spirit of YeHoVaH shall rest upon him, the spirit of wisdom and understanding, the spirit of counsel and might, the spirit of knowledge and of the fear of YeHoVaH; 3 And shall make him of quick understanding in the fear of YeHoVaH: and he shall not judge after the sight of his eyes, neither reprove after the hearing of his ears: 4 But with righteousness shall he judge the poor, and reprove with equity for the meek of the earth: and he shall smite the earth with the rod of his mouth, and with the breath of his lips shall he slay the wicked. 5 And righteousness shall be the girdle of his loins, and faithfulness the girdle of his reins.

As a voice and mirror of her Betrothed, the Bride embraces the mind of Yeshua, functioning within the wisdom, understanding, counsel, might, knowledge and fear of YeHoVaH, as did Yeshua. With her mind united with Yeshua, she has a true fear of YeHoVaH, recognizing her primary accountability to Him for her ways, her

CHAPTER 8
His Weaponry of His Oneness

actions, and her words. She judges not by the sight of her own eyes! She corrects not by what she hears with her own ears, either. This Bride, acting within the oneness of her Betrothed, judges righteously, discerning by the power of the Holy Spirit within. Her hand extends to the poor to judge, admonish and correct. She deals justly and fairly, in all her dealings with humankind. She effectively uses the keys of the Kingdom of God entrusted to her:

Matthew 16:19
19 And I will give unto thee the keys of the kingdom of heaven: and whatsoever thou shalt bind on earth shall be bound[67] in heaven: and whatsoever thou shalt loose on earth shall be loosed in heaven.

In her judgments, the Bride, also, deals with the spiritual foe: As she advances forward with the gospel, she moves in righteous judgment rebuking the powers of darkness, which seek to kill, rob and destroy humankind. At that same time, the Bride extends her loving hand of mercy to those in need. In accordance with

---

[67] A better translation incorporates the tense of this passage to read, has already been bound and has already been loosed.

Yeshua's words, as she preaches the gospel, she forgives or retains the sins of others:[68]

John 20:23
> 23 Whose soever sins ye remit, they are remitted unto them; [and] whose soever [sins] ye retain, they are retained.

THE BRIDE THROUGHOUT THE AGES
While this picture of the Bride outlines her role well, unfortunately, as we look at the Bride throughout the ages, we see where the Bride failed to present this call of her Betrothed. In seasons when the Bride failed, reasons for that failure lay in a disconnect with the scriptures, the Holy Spirit and with fellow believers, also.

Doctrinal statements based on manmade teachings often divided her into segments of religious functions, which, unfortunately, eliminated the heart of her Betrothed from functioning within their intended oneness. Repenting and returning[69] to the Word of God,

---

[68] Those who accept the gospel's message of salvation have their sins forgiven. Those who reject that message have their sins retained!
[69] In other words, Revival!

CHAPTER 8
His Weaponry of His Oneness

realigning to walk in unity with the Holy Spirit, brought healing and restoration.

HIS WEAPON OF HIS ONENESS
While the Bride struggled many times in past seasons, her ability to rise up in Holy Spirit power, presently and in the future, remains. It comes to pass, too, whenever she seeks the Face of her Betrothed. Armed with the knowledge of the Word, which teaches her how to embrace and live out her oneness with her Betrothed, she comes alive again, moving into complete alignment with the Holy Spirit. He in turn, helps to build solid unity within, uniting fellow believers. Thus, the Bride acts as one with each other as well as one with the Living God and so, fulfills her destiny!

Indeed, the Bride, with God's help, mounts up on eagle's wings, demonstrating the oneness of her Betrothed to the world. Her weaponry of His Oneness, once noticed, recognized and embraced, brings her to the forefront as the powerful entity God called into being. Walking in that oneness, as the Bride moves forward, she employs a powerful aspect of heavenly weaponry and thoroughly impacts the earth.

THE WARRIOR BRIDE
Advancing God's Kingdom Through Warfare

Isaiah 40:31

31 But they that wait upon YeHoVaH shall renew [their] strength; they shall mount up with wings as eagles; they shall run, and not be weary; [and] they shall walk, and not faint.

9

HIS WEAPONRY OF HIS AUTHORITY

"And Jesus came and spake unto them, saying, All power [authority] [70]is given unto me in heaven and in earth."

Matthew 28:18

Authority in our day and age means many things, from permission to do a certain thing, to operating a piece of equipment with a governmental license. Authority, as defined within the Bible, including the one above, carries a meaning of making a legally binding decision. In the case of the scripture above, that legally binding decision affects heaven and earth.

---

[70] This word is better interpreted as authority, rather than power.

CHAPTER 9
His Weaponry of His Authority

In Matthew 28:18, Yeshua, Who sits at the right hand of the Father in Heaven, relates to the Apostles His ultimate authority over all things operating in heaven and in earth. All attempts to usurp Yeshua's rule, or even decree *contrary to* Him end in failure because He holds the ultimate authority.[71] This ultimate authority, as the Apostolic scriptures explain, arise from Yeshua's victory on earth and His subsequent appointed position in heaven.

In speaking of that position, Paul the Apostle, petitioned God to help believers understand Yeshua's position and ultimate authority. He requests, on behalf of believers, that God open the eyes of their understanding so they can grasp the greatness of Yeshua. In that way, they can apply His victory on their behalf to their own lives and live according to that truth:

> Ephesians 1:15-23
> 15 ¶ Wherefore I also, after I heard of your faith in the Lord Jesus, and love unto all the saints, 16 Cease not to give thanks for you, making mention of you in my prayers; 17 That the God of our Lord Jesus Christ, the Father of glory, may give unto you the

---
[71] He reserves the right to veto anything contrary His will.

spirit of wisdom and revelation in the knowledge of him: 18 The eyes of your understanding being enlightened; that ye may know what is the hope of his calling, and what the riches of the glory of his inheritance in the saints, 19 And what [is] the exceeding greatness of his power to usward who believe, according to the working of his mighty power, 20 Which he wrought in Christ, when he raised him from the dead, and set [him] at his own right hand in the heavenly [places], 21 Far above all principality, and power, and might, and dominion, and every name that is named, not only in this world, but also in that which is to come: 22 And hath put all [things] under his feet, and gave him [to be] the head over all [things] to the church, 23 Which is his body, the fulness of him that filleth all in all.

Paul rejoices, as those who comprise the Bride, come to faith in Yeshua. He petitions YeHoVaH, the Father of Yeshua, to give every reading and listening[72] audience, wisdom and revelation in the knowledge of God.

---

[72] Some read the letters, while others listened to them.

CHAPTER 9
His Weaponry of His Authority

Paul desires the eyes of their understanding open wide, so that each might know the hope of their unique calling by God, and thus, fully grasp the riches of the inheritance they have in Yeshua. Paul points out the exceeding greatness of God's power[73] towards believers, through the incredible planning of the Father, when YeHoVaH raised Yeshua from the dead and set Him on high in heavenly places,

That place of honour given to the sinless Son of YeHoVaH, Yeshua, towers above every other power known or unknown to man. In addition, YeHoVaH gave Yeshua a name that is above all names, over things in this present world and also in the one which comes later.[74]

No matter the authority, no matter its rank or instituted position, on earth or in heaven, Yeshua's authority looms high above it. YeHoVaH put all things beneath Yeshua's feet. Yeshua is now, and always will be, the head of

---

[73] This word is "dunamis", which is akin to dynamite. It is not authority to which the Apostle refers, here, but rather actual power!

[74] The world when God fully dwells with man upon the earth.

THE WARRIOR BRIDE
Advancing God's Kingdom Through Warfare

the Bride, which is His body, and the fulness of Him and fills all in all! [75]

While all those blessings seem incredible, *even more than enough,* YeHoVaH lavished more! At that same time of Yeshua's exaltation, the Father initiated a shift in the Bride, which placed her into a position in the heavenlies, from where He intends that she functions:

> Ephesians 2:4-10
> 4 ¶ But God, who is rich in mercy, for his great love wherewith he loved us, 5 Even when we were dead in sins, hath quickened us together with Christ, (by grace ye are saved;) 6 And hath raised [us] up together, and made [us] sit together in heavenly [places] in Christ Jesus: 7 That in the ages to come he might shew the exceeding riches of his grace in [his] kindness toward us through Christ Jesus.
> 8 For by grace are ye saved through faith; and that not of yourselves: [it is] the gift of God: 9 Not of works, lest any man should boast. 10 For we are his workmanship,

---

[75] This shows the Bride, once again, as a powerful representation of Yeshua as she lives out her role upon this earth. (Keep in mind the term "Bride" is not gender specific.)

CHAPTER 9
His Weaponry of His Authority

created in Christ Jesus unto good works, which God hath before ordained that we should walk in them.

Shifting the authority to heavenly places, YeHoVaH positioned the Bride to align the things of this earth, which seem to pull away from the truth, with the direction of heaven. With the Holy Spirit's guidance and help, the Bride declares God's truth, pushes back the powers of darkness with a powerful impact and extends salvation to all.

From that impact of that place in the heavenlies, her function on earth gives her opportunity to release commands. Through the power of the Holy Spirit, life changes! Things on earth happen! Unsaved become saved. Sick become healed. Dead become alive, raised to life again! Functioning in these things, the Bride walks in those good works foreordained for her!

Therefore, as the Bride follows in the footsteps of Yeshua, she fulfills a description of what the earth knew must happen when God's Promised One arrived on the scene. With her oneness in Yeshua intact, the Bride continues His ministry responding as Yeshua:

THE WARRIOR BRIDE
Advancing God's Kingdom Through Warfare

Luke 7:22-23

> 22 Then Jesus answering said unto them, Go your way, and tell John what things ye have seen and heard; how that the blind see, the lame walk, the lepers are cleansed, the deaf hear, the dead are raised, to the poor the gospel is preached. 23 And blessed is [he], whosoever shall not be offended in me.

As the Spirit of YeHoVaH directs the Bride she completes the assignment by which she was commissioned:[76]

Matthew 28:18-20

> 18 And Jesus came and spake unto them, saying, All power is given unto me in heaven and in earth. 19 Go ye therefore, and teach all nations, baptizing them in the name of the Father, and of the Son, and of the Holy Ghost: 20 Teaching them to observe all things whatsoever I have commanded you: and, lo, I am with you

---

[76] This word "commissioned" comes from two words, one "co" just as the word we use to suggest joining, e.g., *co*habit. Here, there is *"co"* mission ... Two entities together performing a mission: see lost souls saved!

CHAPTER 9
His Weaponry of His Authority

alway, [even] unto the end of the world. Amen.

UTILIZING AUTHORITY

Fulfilling the command to "go" into all nations, unfortunately, creates much opposition. This aspect the New Testament witnesses as it recorded the lives of the early apostles, who preached the Word. Peter, John and Paul, to name a few, experienced both opposition and imprisonment in their efforts to take the message of salvation to all in their generation. One such experience of the preachers of the gospel, the book of Acts relates:

Acts 16:16-18

16 ¶ And it came to pass, as we went to prayer, a certain damsel possessed with a spirit of divination met us, which brought her masters much gain by soothsaying: 17 The same followed Paul and us, and cried, saying, These men are the servants of the most high God, which shew unto us the way of salvation. 18 And this did she many days. But Paul, being grieved, turned and said to the spirit, I command thee in the name of Jesus Christ to come out of her. And he came out the same hour.

Here, with a word, Paul, through the power of the Holy Spirit, set a woman free of divination. While the woman herself, most likely showed gratitude, her masters did not:

> Acts 16:19-24
>
> 19 And when her masters saw that the hope of their gains was gone, they caught Paul and Silas, and drew [them] into the marketplace unto the rulers, 20 And brought them to the magistrates, saying, These men, being Jews, do exceedingly trouble our city, 21 And teach customs, which are not lawful for us to receive, neither to observe, being Romans. 22 And the multitude rose up together against them: and the magistrates rent off their clothes and commanded to beat [them]. 23 And when they had laid many stripes upon them, they cast [them] into prison, charging the jailor to keep them safely: 24 Who, having received such a charge, thrust them into the inner prison, and made their feet fast in the stocks.

Paul and Silas, in direct response to their good deed, faced an enraged master. Feeling robbed of his income, the woman's master dragged

CHAPTER 9
His Weaponry of His Authority

these preachers of the gospel before a magistrate's court. There they beat Paul and Silas with whips and threw them in jail. While in jail, Paul and Silas, even though their bodies ached from their wounds, employed a weapon of Worship[77].

As they worshipped, YeHoVaH orchestrated their release by causing something miraculous to happen:

> Acts 16:25 -27
> 25 ¶ And at midnight Paul and Silas prayed, and sang praises unto God: and the prisoners heard them. 26 And suddenly there was a great earthquake, so that the foundations of the prison were shaken: and immediately all the doors were opened, and all one's bands were loosed. 27 And the keeper of the prison awaking out of his sleep, and seeing the prison doors open, he drew out his sword, and would have killed himself, supposing that the prisoners had been fled.

---

[77] See Chapter 5 to understand about the weapon of worship.

THE WARRIOR BRIDE
Advancing God's Kingdom Through Warfare

Miraculously, YeHoVaH saw to the opening of the prison doors by causing an earthquake. As the earth shook, the doors opened. Those prisoners for the gospel's sake, thrust into the deepest part of the prison, could now escape. In fear, the jailer, knowing Rome's death penalty to come upon him for allowing prisoners to escape, decided to take his own life. He drew his sword and positioned it, ready to kill himself.

Acts 16:28-34

28 But Paul cried with a loud voice, saying, Do thyself no harm: for we are all here. 29 Then he called for a light, and sprang in, and came trembling, and fell down before Paul and Silas, 30 And brought them out, and said, Sirs, what must I do to be saved? 31 And they said, Believe on the Lord Jesus Christ, and thou shalt be saved, and thy house. 32 And they spake unto him the word of the Lord, and to all that were in his house. 33 And he took them the same hour of the night and washed [their] stripes; and was baptized, he and all his, straightway. 34 And when he had brought them into his house, he set meat before them, and rejoiced, believing in God with all his house.

CHAPTER 9
His Weaponry of His Authority

Paul and Silas, in compassion and love, reached out to the jailer. They informed him that no prisoners escaped, and thus, his life was not in jeopardy. Recognizing the hand of God with Paul and Silas, the jailer, grateful and respectful of Paul and Silas, inquired how he might be saved. After sharing the gospel, the jailer and all his house entered God's Kingdom.

HIS WEAPON OF HIS AUTHORITY
In this amazing testimony of God's greatness, we see many weapons used, not against the human beings within the story but rather, in the background. Paul and Silas, under the magistrate's authority, suffered beating and imprisonment; nevertheless, they drew from their arsenal of spiritual weapons, God's Weapon of His Worship.

As a result, by an act of God, the earth quaked, the prison doors opened. Heaven's authority overturned that of man! Paul and Silas received their freedom. Afterwards, with no escape taking place, the jailer retained his life. Weaponry of the Good News[78], which showed

---

[78] Explained in a later Chapter.

God desired no harm to this jailer, produced a crop of saved souls for the Kingdom of God.

ALL WEAPONRY
This marvellous compilation of weaponry moved heaven to act on behalf of earth. Weaponry of His Worship, such as using His Name, His Word, and His Authority[79] produces incredible outcomes, all geared to advancing the Kingdom of God. The Warrior Bride, learning to use her weaponry of heaven, *as God directs*, sees heaven's plan realized upon the earth: Walking in sync with Her Betrothed, she rejoices as His Kingdom Comes, as His Will is Done!

---

[79] In this Chapter, the Bride did not use the authority, directly, but Heaven expects her to do so as the need arises.

10

HIS WEAPONRY OF HIS DOMINION

"Consume [them] in wrath, consume [them], that they [may] not [be]: and let them know that God ruleth in Jacob unto the ends of the earth. Selah."

Psalm 59:13

In escaping from King Saul who sought his life, King David took comfort in the knowledge that YeHoVaH ruled in Israel, and even to the ends of the earth. Later, one of his descendants, Daniel, who Babylon took into captivity, related the same message of God's ability to rule over the earth:

Daniel 4: 17

17 This matter [is] by the decree of the watchers, and the demand by the word of the holy ones: to the intent that the living may know that the most High ruleth in the kingdom of men, and giveth it to

CHAPTER 10
His Weaponry of His Dominion

whomsoever he will, and setteth up over it the basest of men.

To recognize the dominion of YeHoVaH brings much with it, including a peace that the One Who created the universe does not abandon it. We see that, clearly, as we look at the Hebrew root interpreted as "ruleth"[80].

Strong's # 4910 "Rules"	מָשַׁל Pronounced: maw-shal'
Meaning: to rule, have dominion, reign, to exercise dominion	

This same idea of ruling Moses spoke about as he recorded how YeHoVaH gave Adam and Eve dominion in the Garden of Eden before sin entered the world. In Genesis we read that YeHoVaH placed Adam and Eve in their place of dominion over the earth for the purpose of subduing it, even doing so over the fish of the sea; over the fowl of the air, and over every living thing that moved upon the earth:

---

[80] It is the same Hebrew word in Psalm 59:13; Daniel 4:17, 25, 32.

THE WARRIOR BRIDE
Advancing God's Kingdom Through Warfare

Genesis 1:28

> "And God blessed them, and God said unto them, Be fruitful, and multiply, and replenish the earth, and subdue it: and have dominion over the fish of the sea, and over the fowl of the air, and over every living thing that moveth upon the earth."

However, as residents of this earth ourselves, we know more components of earth exist than those listed in Genesis 1:28. This planet of earth experiences elements of nature such as the wind, or waves of the seas. God did not release the dominion of these to Adam. Other elements exist, too. He retained His rulership over the expanse of the heavens, including the sun, moon, stars and planets. What God retained, He did so in Adam's day, and it still remains, today.

While Adam, through disobedience, lost his dominion, Yeshua regained it for humankind. Since the cross and Yeshua's great victory, dominion regained by Yeshua remains in His Name, however, due to the Bride's positioning in the heavenlies, she has access to that dominion. Such a great salvation as ours, which brings with it such access, authority and power,

CHAPTER 10
His Weaponry of His Dominion

gives glory to the One through Whom YeHoVaH made all things, namely, Yeshua.

Hebrews 1:1-4

1 ¶ God, who at sundry times and in divers manners spake in time past unto the fathers by the prophets, 2 Hath in these last days spoken unto us by [his] Son, whom he hath appointed heir of all things, by whom also he made the worlds; 3 Who being the brightness of [his] glory, and the express image of his person, and upholding all things by the word of his power, when he had by himself purged our sins, sat down on the right hand of the Majesty on high; 4 ¶ Being made so much better than the angels, as he hath by inheritance obtained a more excellent name than they.

Yeshua's dominion over the earth and over all things, including nature and the heavenlies, becomes a good thing to keep in mind when trouble arises. Additionally, the knowledge of this dominion and *the exercise* of it, brings much wisdom to the Bride as she moves ahead to implement the strategies God assigned to her to attain her destiny.

This knowledge of the weaponry of His Dominion, which is the topic of this chapter, helps to make the Bride victorious over the works of ha satan. Mindsets of the Bride, which align with this dominion, elevate her confidence to the proper level of trust needed for victory.

DOMINION OVER DEATH

Yeshua, through His glorious resurrection, showed the world that death has no dominion over Him, rather Yeshua has dominion over death:

> Romans 6:9
> 9 Knowing that Christ being raised from the dead dieth no more; death hath no more dominion over him

One day Yeshua will end that death's dominion for all those who believe in Him[81]. That is His promise! Indeed, death lies beneath the feet of Yeshua! He conquered it and the grave!

> 1 Corinthians 15:52-57
> 52 In a moment, in the twinkling of an eye, at the last trump: for the trumpet shall sound, and the dead shall be raised

---

[81] John 11:26 And whosoever liveth and believeth in me shall never die. Believest thou this?

CHAPTER 10
His Weaponry of His Dominion

incorruptible, and we shall be changed. 53 For this corruptible must put on incorruption, and this mortal [must] put on immortality.

54 So when this corruptible shall have put on incorruption, and this mortal shall have put on immortality, then shall be brought to pass the saying that is written, Death is swallowed up in victory. 55 O death, where [is] thy sting? O grave, where [is] thy victory? 56 The sting of death [is] sin; and the strength of sin [is] the law. 57 But thanks [be] to God, which giveth us the victory through our Lord Jesus Christ.

To the Bride, Yeshua gave commandments to raise the dead, thus using His dominion to demonstrate the Kingdom of God's reality:

Matthew 10:7-8[82]

7 And as ye go, preach, saying, The kingdom of heaven is at hand. 8 Heal the sick, cleanse the lepers, raise the dead, cast out devils: freely ye have received, freely give.

DOMINION OVER SIN

---

[82] While this command came before the cross, it was reiterated after the cross, also!

THE WARRIOR BRIDE
Advancing God's Kingdom Through Warfare

As the Bride moves ahead implementing the dominion found in her Betrothed, she enjoys another benefit of belonging to the One Who conquered the grave:

Romans 6:14
> 14 For sin shall not have dominion over you: for ye are not under the law, but under grace.

This amazing truth, which the Bride experiences, lives by and preaches, breaks the chains and bonds of ha satan.

Trusting in Yeshua for salvation, and for total deliverance, the Bride rejoices that sin no longer rules those in Yeshua. The good news, here, is that the Bride, equipped by God and walking in her dominion promises freedom from sin and through the power of the Holy Spirit, sees those who desire freedom receive it! What a weapon of dominion to use against the snares and traps of ha satan![83]

---

[83] We'll look more into preaching the good news as a weapon of warfare, later in the book.

CHAPTER 10
His Weaponry of His Dominion

DOMINION OVER NATURE

As Yeshua walked upon this earth, He demonstrated His power over nature. His disciples saw that dominion manifested over the wild winds and raging storm they faced in the Sea of Galilee:

> Mark 4:36-41
>> 36 And when they had sent away the multitude, they took him even as he was in the ship. And there were also with him other little ships. 37 And there arose a great storm of wind, and the waves beat into the ship, so that it was now full. 38 And he was in the hinder part of the ship, asleep on a pillow: and they awake him, and say unto him, Master, carest thou not that we perish? 39 And he arose, and rebuked the wind, and said unto the sea, Peace, be still. And the wind ceased, and there was a great calm. 40 And he said unto them, Why are ye so fearful? how is it that ye have no faith? 41 And they feared exceedingly, and said one to another, What manner of man is this, that even the wind and the sea obey him?

In another place, we see Yeshua walking on the water:

THE WARRIOR BRIDE
Advancing God's Kingdom Through Warfare

Mark 14:23-27
> 23 And when he had sent the multitudes away, he went up into a mountain apart to pray: and when the evening was come, he was there alone. 24 But the ship was now in the midst of the sea, tossed with waves: for the wind was contrary. 25 And in the fourth watch of the night Jesus went unto them, walking on the sea. 26 And when the disciples saw him walking on the sea, they were troubled, saying, It is a spirit; and they cried out for fear. 27 But straightway Jesus spake unto them, saying, Be of good cheer; it is I; be not afraid.

Knowing her Betrothed never changes, the Bride looks to Him for the miraculous whenever it is needed. He, then, does as He needs to do! He either calms the seas or helps the Bride weather the storm. Remembering His dominion helps the Bride to stay focused on her Betrothed's ability. She knows He'll respond for He will never forsake her!

POWER OVER NATIONS
According to our opening verse and 3 other verifiable sources of the Word, God rules in the

CHAPTER 10
His Weaponry of His Dominion

kingdom of men[84]. While to the mind of man ruling nations seems to be a big deal, God perceives it differently:

> Isaiah 40:17
> "All nations before him [are] as nothing; and they are counted to him less than nothing, and vanity."

Whether the Bride *(or others)* agree or disagree with a nation's choice of leadership, God still rules in the Kingdom of men. Scripture says it; therefore, it is truth. For the Bride, her mind must focus on her Betrothed's dominion remembering that He knows the entirely of the circumstances, with a deep and intricate knowledge of personal and corporate outcomes that man cannot begin to perceive.

Thus, as the Bride implements her Betrothed's plans upon this earth, she remembers His Dominion. That dominion, the Bride, in humility with a confidence of a response, seeks

---

[84] Some believers interpret this to mean that, in Messiah, all events come to pass through avenues of their choice, *seeing God's reign only over that which man releases to Him.* Others believe God rules sovereignly in the kingdom of men, with or without man's permission to do so. This author believes the latter.

THE WARRIOR BRIDE
Advancing God's Kingdom Through Warfare

the will of her Betrothed. He reveals His will, accordingly, declaring it for her to understand. Her Beloved, well able to bring that will to come to pass, does so, in the timeframe, and manner of His choice.

In reflecting on the Bride's history, over the centuries, many times she suffered indignities at the hands of brutal men. Nevertheless, she arose unscathed from that persecution. Scripture, unfortunately, does not detail the defining line of His Betrothed's deliverance, however, it gives us a clue to help understand:

> Hebrews 11:32-40
> 32 And what shall I more say? for the time would fail me to tell of Gedeon, and [of] Barak, and [of] Samson, and [of] Jephthae; [of] David also, and Samuel, and [of] the prophets: 33 Who through faith subdued kingdoms, wrought righteousness, obtained promises, stopped the mouths of lions, 34 Quenched the violence of fire, escaped the edge of the sword, out of weakness were made strong, waxed valiant in fight, turned to flight the armies of the aliens. 35 Women received their dead raised to life again: and others were

CHAPTER 10
His Weaponry of His Dominion

tortured, not accepting deliverance; that they might obtain a better resurrection: 36 And others had trial of [cruel] mockings and scourgings, yea, moreover of bonds and imprisonment: 37 They were stoned, they were sawn asunder, were tempted, were slain with the sword: they wandered about in sheepskins and goatskins; being destitute, afflicted, tormented; 38 (Of whom the world was not worthy:) they wandered in deserts, and [in] mountains, and [in] dens and caves of the earth. 39 And these all, having obtained a good report through faith, received not the promise: 40 God having provided some better thing for us, that they without us should not be made perfect.

This phrase, *"God providing some better things"*, gives the clue to understanding why persecution and what earth might consider a failure, happens to the Bride. This does not bring a negative slant to God's Dominion for it is in place, and He knows the outcome. He understands the greater picture, how it fits together, and how in eternity, the results play out. In reality, the Bride cannot afford to focus on anything other than the better kingdom scripture promises.

Hebrews 11:13-16
> 13 These all died in faith, not having received the promises, but having seen them afar off, and were persuaded of [them], and embraced [them], and confessed that they were strangers and pilgrims on the earth. 14 For they that say such things declare plainly that they seek a country. 15 And truly, if they had been mindful of that [country] from whence they came out, they might have had opportunity to have returned. 16 But now they desire a better [country], that is, an heavenly: wherefore God is not ashamed to be called their God: for he hath prepared for them a city.

This does not negate, in any way, God's dominion, nor the Bride's trust in it. Rather, it reinforces it, for His watchful eye looks beyond the "flesh", beyond the circumstances of the day to the greater benefit of living eternally with Him.

CHAPTER 10
His Weaponry of His Dominion

HIS WEAPON OF DOMINION

Therefore, as the Bride fulfills her mandate upon the earth, she rejoices in her Betrothed's dominion, over all things. She asks His help in looing beyond the immediate scope of today, to look at the greater picture, which includes a promising tomorrow! She trusts in His perfect plan for her and does her best to fulfill her part of that plan. Daily, step by step, as the Bride walks along, she believes and declares that very dominion of her Betrothed. He rules over ha satan, over the kingdom of men, over all things which rise up against His plans and purposes.

Likewise, she seeks His Face to understand His will in all things. In doing so, she remembers that her members are but flesh and blood. Focusing and trusting in His dominion brings a peace and confidence in the One with Whom she will spend her future. The Dominion of God, when remembered, spoken about and utilized, keeps the Bride focused on Him, and the future when she spends eternity with Him in that "better country" of which scripture speaks. That is a great weapon, and too valuable to overlook!

THE WARRIOR BRIDE
Advancing God's Kingdom Through Warfare

"Lay not up for yourselves treasures upon earth, where moth and rust doth corrupt, and where thieves break through and steal: But lay up for yourselves treasures in heaven, where neither moth nor rust doth corrupt, and where thieves do not break through nor steal: For where your treasure is, there will your heart be also."

Matthew 6:19-21

CONCLUSION OF SECTION 2, PART 1

This section of the book, which focused on the first part of the Bride's Creed: To Love our God, listed and explained some of the weaponry available to the Bride:
- His Weaponry of His Worship,
- His Weaponry of His Name
- His Weaponry of His Word
- His Weaponry of His Oneness
- His Weaponry of His Authority
- His Weaponry of His Dominion

This list, by no means includes all of the weaponry given to the Bride. Other weapons exist, such as His Weaponry of His Knowledge, His Weaponry of His Compassion, Mercy and Love. Additionally, there His weaponry of His Presence makes a considerable impact as the

CHAPTER 10
His Weaponry of His Dominion

Bride's Betrothed goes with her. The list goes on and on! Whatever aspects of the weaponry the Bride employs on behalf of humankind, she does so by drawing nearer to her Betrothed, Who teaches and releases to her all that benefits humankind.

In leaving this part of the book, *(Section 2, Part 1, To Love our God)*, recall the Bride's deeply rooted, unadulterated love for her Betrothed. Note her focused, single eyed relationship with her Betrothed, which never shifts away, *not even for a moment*, to gaze at another. In addition, consider the Bride, when functioning in Holy Spirit power, never reverts to tools of the flesh, which produce nothing of eternal value. Rather, the Bride employs the weaponry, and mindsets of her Betrothed, as the Holy Spirit leads and thus, does the work of the Kingdom. All her weaponry employed fall into the same category as mighty through God to the pulling down of strongholds.[85] Their implementation makes an immense impact in the present world in which she lives.

---

[85] 2 Corinthians 10:4 (For the weapons of our warfare [are] not carnal, but mighty through God to the pulling down of strong holds;)

Also, keep in mind that when the individual members who make up the Bride err, *either in judgment, exercising His Will, or living their own personal life,* the Betrothed provides forgiveness and cleansing for her. So that on the day she sees Him face to face, she is purified, having made herself ready:

"Let us be glad and rejoice and give honour to him: for the marriage of the Lamb is come, and his wife hath made herself ready." (Revelation 19:7)

SECTION 2

THE BRIDE MOBILIZED

Part 2: To Love Our Neighbour

11

HIS WEAPONRY OF HIS GOSPEL

"For I am not ashamed of the gospel of Christ: for it is the power of God unto salvation to everyone that believeth; to the Jew first, and also to the Greek. For therein is the righteousness of God revealed from faith to faith: as it is written, The just shall live by faith."

Romans 1:16-17

Most people love to hear good news, and as such open their ears to hear it. Thus, the Bride, in her expression of the good news from heaven, or the gospel as we call it, points to an awesome door to change people's lives. If a listener receives that message and walks through that open door, therein lies endless opportunities to receive God's best for their lives. That best, while including gifts for the future, includes a present time experience,

CHAPTER 11
His Weaponry of His Gospel

part of which includes the embrace of the Bride's Beloved Who reaches out to touch the hurting people of this world, including them.

Unfortunately, not everyone recognizes, acknowledges and then accepts the importance of the gospel or its relevance to touch broken people, either Jew or Gentile. Thus, some fail to perceive its message of hope for today and its lifeline for tomorrow. Such mindsets refuse to open their hearts to receive the gospel message. Nevertheless, the Bride preaches, as the measuring stick for using the gospel message is not *its reception*, but rather *its proclamation*.

2 Timothy 4:1-2
1 I charge [thee] therefore before God, and the Lord Jesus Christ, who shall judge the quick and the dead at his appearing and his kingdom; 2 Preach the word; be instant in season, out of season; reprove, rebuke, exhort with all longsuffering and doctrine.

No matter the season for the gospel, (in or out of season), the Bride remembers that the gospel's message received its design from God. While its main focus reaches out to touch the human beings of this world, behind the scenes, its power moves and removes the spiritual forces of darkness which keep people in bondage. It challenges the very one that tries to keep humankind in its ugly grasp:

> 2 Corinthians 4:3-7
> 3 But if our gospel he hid, it is hid to them that are lost: 4 In whom the god of this world hath blinded the minds of them which believe not, lest the light of the glorious gospel of Christ, who is the image of God, should shine unto them. 5 For we preach not ourselves, but Christ Jesus the Lord; and ourselves your servants for Jesus' sake. 6 For God, who commanded the light to shine out of darkness, hath shined in our hearts, to [give] the light of the knowledge of the glory of God in the face of Jesus Christ. 7 But we have this treasure in earthen vessels, that the excellency of the power may be of God, and not of us.

In this passage, the author, Paul the Apostle, speaks about the light the gospel sheds for humankind to receive. Such light brings the knowledge of the glory of God. Its power touches hearts. In addition, Paul speaks of a certain blindness that clouds the minds of those

CHAPTER 11
His Weaponry of His Gospel

who do not believe. That blindness originates in ha satan, who, in this passage, Paul addresses as "the god of this world". [86]

Indeed, as ha satan employs his tactics to blind the minds of those who disbelieve, the gospel message has an inherent power. That power challenges and shatters the blindness. All it takes is a person's agreement with the Word of God. Once that agreement happens, ha satan's blindness operates no further. The light dawns! At which time, ha satan's work meets with a shattering and disannulling force, unlocking prison doors and setting captives free. This inherent power rests within the gospel message!

**The gospel's goal:
undo the works of ha satan!**

Those works, Yeshua recapped:

John 10:9-11

9 I am the door: by me if any man enter in, he shall be saved, and shall go in and out, and find pasture. 10 The thief cometh not, but for to steal, and to kill, and to destroy:

---

[86] Paul uses this to show that ha satan has *an influential power **over the unsaved**.* Paul's words do not convey a message that *the god of this world,* ha satan, *rules it!*

THE WARRIOR BRIDE
Advancing God's Kingdom Through Warfare

I am come that they might have life, and that they might have [it] more abundantly. 11 I am the good shepherd: the good shepherd giveth his life for the sheep.

Here, Yeshua addresses ha satan as a thief who comes to steal, kill and destroy. Thus, these seen in a person's life, means only one thing: ha satan's works. Yeshua teaches with authority and clarity, such works point to ha satan as the source, not to God! For some, those words of Yeshua, hit a cord. Many people thought bad things happened because of God's displeasure. Yeshua taught otherwise.

Yeshua, God incarnate, came to bring life, *and abundantly*. God's love for humankind proved itself immense as He sent Yeshua to bring that abundant life to reality for those who desired it. Therefore, when the Bride speaks forth the gospel message and encounters individuals snared by the works of ha satan, she implements her weaponry to the source of the problem:

Ephesians 6:12
12 For we wrestle not against flesh and blood, but against principalities, against powers, against the rulers of the darkness

CHAPTER 11
His Weaponry of His Gospel

of this world, against spiritual wickedness in high [places].

While the Bride's message reaches out to humankind, her warfare weaponry which God designed for her, hits ha satan and his powers of darkness hidden in the background.

With ha satan removed from the scene, with his powers broken by the authority of God's Word and Name, humankind have a better opportunity to hear the truth. After that, they decide to agree or disagree with it. Some chose to align with truth and live in the light, while others prefer to keep their alignment with ha satan and thus, live in darkness.

As the Bride preaches the gospel, she cannot hold opinions on the people to whom she preached. She recognizes that some receive now, some receive later, and some may never receive. For those who receive her message, today, she rejoices. For those who rejected her message today, she prays, hoping they will receive tomorrow.

For those who refuse, altogether, they chose to refuse. While the Bride grieves, she obeys the voice of the Yeshua who advised her to shake the dust off her feet and move on:

Matthew 10:14
14 And whosoever shall not receive you, nor hear your words, when ye depart out of that house or city, shake off the dust of your feet.

People, by God's ordained privilege, own the right to make choices and live with their consequences. Thus, the Bride presents the gospel message, does all the Holy Spirit instructs, then leaves the rest with YeHoVaH, including any opposition she may receive.

Regarding opposition, in the life of the Apostle Paul, we hear of someone who deliberately and intentionally withstood Paul to prevent a person from receiving the gospel.

Acts 13:5-12
5 And when they were at Salamis, they preached the word of God in the synagogues of the Jews: and they had also John to [their] minister. 6 And when they had gone through the isle unto Paphos, they found a certain sorcerer, a false prophet, a Jew, whose name [was]

CHAPTER 11
His Weaponry of His Gospel

Barjesus: 7 Which was with the deputy of the country, Sergius Paulus, a prudent man, who called for Barnabas and Saul, and desired to hear the word of God. 8 But Elymas the sorcerer (for so is his name by interpretation) withstood them, seeking to turn away the deputy from the faith. 9 Then Saul, (who also [is called] Paul,) filled with the Holy Ghost, set his eyes on him, 10 And said, O full of all subtilty and all mischief, [thou] child of the devil, [thou] enemy of all righteousness, wilt thou not cease to pervert the right ways of the Lord? 11 And now, behold, the hand of the Lord [is] upon thee, and thou shalt be blind, not seeing the sun for a season. And immediately there fell on him a mist and a darkness; and he went about seeking some to lead him by the hand. 12 Then the deputy, when he saw what was done, believed, being astonished at the doctrine of the Lord.

In this encounter, we hear of an official, a deputy named Sergius Paulus, who knew a Jewish man named Barjesus. Barjesus, as the book of Acts describes him, obviously lived outside of the Torah, for Paul described him as a sorcerer and a false prophet.[87] From the text, we hear that Barjesus gave counsel to the deputy, Sergius Paulus. Through the influence of Barjesus, Sergius Paulus summoned Paul and Barnabas to come speak the Word of God to them.

As this scene transpired, another sorcerer comes upon the scene; the man named Elymas. He deliberately and intentionally withstood Paul and Barnabas. Elymas determined to turn Sergius Paulus away from the faith. In response to this interference, Paul, filled with the Holy Spirit, set his eyes on Elymas. Out of Paul's mouth comes these words as we saw before:

Acts 13:10-11
> 10 And said, O full of all subtilty and all mischief, [thou] child of the devil, [thou] enemy of all righteousness, wilt thou not cease to pervert the right ways of the Lord? 11 And now, behold, the hand of the Lord [is] upon thee, and thou shalt be blind, not seeing the sun for a season. And

---

[87] Paul reasoned at the synagogue regarding the gospel message. Barjesus as a Jew, most likely, heard the message and passed it on to the official who was with the deputy.

CHAPTER 11
His Weaponry of His Gospel

immediately there fell on him a mist and a darkness; and he went about seeking some to lead him by the hand.

As a direct result, Elymas walked away blinded, looking for someone to help him. When the deputy saw what happened to Elymas, being astonished at the doctrine of the Lord, he believed.

This event resulted in the salvation of the deputy but, unfortunately, it saw a temporary blindness for the sorcerer, Elymas. Some, in reading this event in the books of Acts, think Paul reacted too strongly to the opposition to the gospel message, however, the Spirit relates this incident to us for a good reason. Paul's response to Elymas, did not originate in the flesh, but in the Holy Spirit. **Let's read it again**:

Acts 13:9-11
9 Then Saul, (who also [is called] Paul,) filled with the Holy Ghost, set his eyes on him, 10 And said, O full of all subtilty and all mischief, [thou] child of the devil, [thou] enemy of all righteousness, wilt thou not cease to pervert the right ways of the Lord? 11 And now, behold, the hand of the Lord

[is] upon thee, and thou shalt be blind, not seeing the sun for a season. And immediately there fell on him a mist and a darkness; and he went about seeking some to lead him by the hand.

Since the action came by the Holy Spirit infilling Paul, we know a deeper reason exists for the blindness of Elymas.

When the power of the Holy Spirit fell upon Elymas, his physical body experienced what his spiritual mind did not recognize: *his blindness.* Elymas, whom Paul commanded blind for a season, experienced a greater power than ever before in his lifetime. He now experienced the power of the living God, Who far surpassed the spiritual realm of ha satan, with whom Elymas associated and served. Indeed, through this temporary act of blindness, God showed Elymas his own spiritual blindness. Thus, *Elymas received God's mercy, not judgment!*

This blindness, which came *for a season,* gave time for Elymas to reflect upon the error of his ways, as well as the superior power of the God Paul served. Elymas' temporary blindness came not to punish nor to destroy him! That

CHAPTER 11
His Weaponry of His Gospel

blindness came to cause Elymas to question his choices in life and give him an open door to receive Paul's message of salvation.

While the Bible does not tell us the result of this temporary blindness in the life of Elymas, it does speak about another man who received a temporary blindness, which did result in his salvation. This man, who opposed the preaching of the gospel and demonstrated it in murderous ways, was none other than the very apostle[88] standing in front of Elymas, giving the command for blindness! Perhaps, in Paul's mind, Elymas seemed a likely candidate to receive what he, himself received.

So, while the Bible does not directly reveal any intentions of Paul, we know that his action originated in the power of the Holy Spirit and evidently manifested for the good of Elymas, giving him opportunity to take a road leading to truth.

Additionally, this action manifested another thing, *an act of mercy to Sergius Paulus.*

---

[88] Acts 9:8

ABOUT SERGIUS PAULUS

Sergius Paulus, in his time of office in Rome, functioned as deputy over a region. His interest in Paul in the gospel message opened a door for him to receive salvation. After his powerful salvation, positive changes must have happened in his life, family and job. As a government official in the region, his salvation, probably, affected the very court system of that area, as Sergius Paulus influence as he went about doing his duties. For all we know, this salvation may have been a key salvation to break many chains of darkness within that region and set the captive people free.

LESSONS FROM THIS INCIDENT

Deeper issues of Elymas' salvation and the future life of Sergius Paulus, the Bible does not relate. However, a message we definitely hear by the record of this event, shows the supremacy of the gospel over the works of darkness. We see God's merciful hand on Elymas and Sergius Paulus. Additionally, we see God, by the power of the Holy Spirit, gave the Apostle Paul all that he needed to preach the gospel, effectively.

CHAPTER 11
His Weaponry of His Gospel

Looking at Paul's response to Elymas, we see a powerful lesson. Paul met the opposition to the gospel, not in the flesh, (not out of anger, nor retaliation), but rather by the power of the Holy Spirit! Indeed, this is an amazing lesson for the Bride! God knows the purpose and the results of every encounter, every resistance to the Word of Truth. The Bride sets her eyes, ears, and heart on her Beloved's guidance through the Holy Spirit and departs not from it! The Bride remembers Who works with her: *The Holy Spirit!*[89]

Truly, the inherent power in the gospel, as YeHoVaH designed, makes the preaching of the Gospel a powerful weapon! Its impact shatters the darkness, opens prison's doors and sets the captives free!

HIS WEAPONRY OF HIS GOSPEL
When the gospel message comes to the ears of humankind, many withstand the gospel message. Those who resist the gospel use their own philosophies and spiritual experiences, which seem very logical to them, to measure the gospel's impact in their life, however, those

---
[89] Mark 16:20

measuring sticks which form their mindsets usually do not agree with the truth, according to the Word of God.

All resistance to the gospel, whether from the natural world of man, or from its spiritual root of darkness, must meet with the hand of the Living God in the manner in which God decrees. Who knows! Maybe one day, the resistant person may turn and agree with God, resulting in their salvation. This is God's intent for them, and whatever He implements on their behalf, this goal is kept in mind.

For the Bride preaching the message, she follows His lead and leaves the results with Him. Thus, as the Bride expresses the gospel, her goal culminates in the rich harvest of souls which come into the Kingdom of God. Indeed, she lives to serve and in service to Her Beloved preaches a loving, kind message aimed at offering forgiveness for sins to all who would receive.

To put her message in simple words, she declares how man breaks God's Laws and commandments. Such choices invite spiritual darkness and eternal death, as well as

CHAPTER 11
His Weaponry of His Gospel

consequences in this world which snare, entrap and imprison humankind. Due to God's mercy, when people receive God's provided Redeemer their chains fall away. Their blindness, which originated from the god of this world dissipates as they learn to receive the truth and align with it. God's gospel, which He designed as a gift to humankind, becomes a powerful tool to set people free to live a better life here, as well as for all eternity, when their life ends.

By confronting darkness and by extending God's plan of forgiveness to listening ears, the gospel brings an anointment to the pain of life, on one hand; and on the other hand, it becomes a weapon of warfare to disengage ha satan in a person's life and opens a door for his prisoners to go free!

This is good news indeed for those who recognize the truth. When they do, and accept God's plan for them, they receive hope, a future and an expected end. Indeed, it is a message of good news! His Weaponry of His Gospel, with its inherent power, has the potential to change everything!

THE WARRIOR BRIDE
Advancing God's Kingdom Through Warfare

"For I know the thoughts that I think toward you, saith YeHoVaH, thoughts of peace, and not of evil, to give you an expected end."

Jeremiah 29:11

12

HIS WEAPONRY OF HIS COMING

"The Spirit of the Lord GOD [is] upon me; because YeHoVaH hath anointed me to preach good tidings unto the meek; he hath sent me to bind up the brokenhearted, to proclaim liberty to the captives, and the opening of the prison to [them that are] bound; To proclaim the acceptable year of YeHoVaH, and the day of vengeance of our God; to comfort all that mourn; To appoint unto them that mourn in Zion, to give unto them beauty for ashes, the oil of joy for mourning, the garment of praise for the spirit of heaviness; that they might be called trees of righteousness, the planting of YeHoVaH, that he might be glorified."

Isaiah 61:1-3

CHAPTER 12
His Weaponry of His Coming

Yeshua stood and read this scripture passage in a synagogue in Nazareth to His Jewish brethren. He stopped at the words, "to preach the acceptable year of YeHoVaH." Then, He sat down[90] with all eyes upon Him. He then said, "This day is this scripture fulfilled in your ears[91]."

Why did He have their attention? Perhaps, the audience wondered why, in this passage, which referred to the coming Messiah, Yeshua excluded "the day of vengeance of our God".

Yeshua, with the wisdom God gave Him, understood that at His First coming, He came as Saviour, Redeemer. When He ended the scripture passage after "the acceptable day of YeHoVaH", He indicated there were two full occasions of His Coming. While those listening to Yeshua did not grasp that message, it became clear later on, and those with ears to hear today, understand its application without hesitation.

Yeshua's first mission, *specifically addressed as "the acceptable year of YeHoVaH", became clear,* as understanding built regarding Yeshua's mission. His exact mission the angel exclaimed:

---

[90] Luke 4:16-20
[91] Luke 4:21

To Mary (Miriam) the angel said:

Luke 1:30-33

> 30 And the angel said unto her, Fear not, Mary: for thou hast found favour with God. 31 And, behold, thou shalt conceive in thy womb, and bring forth a son, and shalt call his name JESUS. 32 He shall be great and shall be called the Son of the Highest: and the Lord God shall give unto him the throne of his father David: 33 And he shall reign over the house of Jacob for ever; and of his kingdom there shall be no end.

When speaking of Yeshua to this beloved woman, who found favour with YeHoVaH, the angel specifically mentioned, *the throne of His Father, David*. Yeshua, destined to sit upon the throne of King David, must stem from the seed of David. Furthermore, this ruler must come out of the specific line of David, which God destined for that throne, namely through the line of Solomon. Mary, (Miriam) who gave birth to Yeshua came from that line.[92]

---

[92] Shown in the linage from the book of Matthew Chapter 1. Joseph, the "father" of Mary, is how the original Hebrew text reads. {KJV errs when it says, "husband" of

CHAPTER 12
His Weaponry of His Coming

To Joseph (Yoseph) the angel said:
Matthew 1:20-21

> 20 But while he thought on these things, behold, the angel of the Lord appeared unto him in a dream, saying, Joseph, thou son of David, fear not to take unto the Mary thy wife: for that which is conceived in her is of the Holy Ghost. 21 And she shall bring forth a son, and thou shalt call his name JESUS: for he shall save his people from their sins.

In tracing Joseph's (Yoseph's) lineage, the man assigned by God to be Mary's (Miriam) husband and Yeshua's stepfather, *also* came from the line of David[93], *but* not from the kingly line of Solomon. Yoseph came from the lineage of another son of David, named Nathan. This explains why Yoseph heard of *Yeshua's mission as Saviour*, not his royal lineage. [94]

Mary.} See "The Chronological Gospels" by Michael Rood, page 44-46.

[93] Luke 3:31

[94] Yoseph, who acted as a father to Yeshua, did not father Him. Yeshua came from the seed of the woman, the virgin espoused to Yoseph.

With these two angelic messages, God made His point:

1. Yeshua came to save His people from their sins, and
2. Yeshua would sit upon the throne of His Father, David. "

These two purposes, however, God destined to be fulfilled in two separate stages. Yeshua's purpose on earth, commissioned before His birth, set Him to be Saviour. In such a manner, then, He lived His life. At Yeshua's death, offered as the Lamb of God, He brought salvation to all who'd receive Him, Jew or Gentile. Later, when returning to His Father, His next coming became clear:

Acts 1:6-11
6 ¶ When they therefore were come together, they asked of him, saying, Lord, wilt thou at this time restore again the kingdom to Israel? 7 And he said unto them, It is not for you to know the times or the seasons, which the Father hath put in his own power. 8 But ye shall receive power, after that the Holy Ghost is come upon you: and ye shall be witnesses unto

CHAPTER 12
His Weaponry of His Coming

me both in Jerusalem, and in all Judaea, and in Samaria, and unto the uttermost part of the earth. 9 And when he had spoken these things, while they beheld, he was taken up; and a cloud received him out of their sight. 10 And while they looked stedfastly toward heaven as he went up, behold, two men stood by them in white apparel; 11 Which also said, Ye men of Galilee, why stand ye gazing up into heaven? this same Jesus, which is taken up from you into heaven, shall so come in like manner as ye have seen him go into heaven.

At Yeshua's first coming, Yeshua did not establish the Kingdom of God in the way that man expected. While Yeshua brought in the Kingdom of God in a manner, *unexpected,* for that Kingdom comes upon people when they hear the gospel message.[95] It is theirs to accept or reject. If they accept, the Kingdom of God moves within. This is not the way the Jews expected it, however, **this is way the message came as Yeshua fulfilled His commission for the acceptable year of YeHoVaH!**

---

[95] Principle of Luke 11:20

When Yeshua walked the earth, King David's throne, from which all legal kings of Israel descend, temporarily sat unoccupied. Rome, instead, sat in a place of governance in Israel. However, Yeshua came not to restore that throne, at that time. Rather, He told the disciples: "It is not for you to know the times or the seasons, which the Father hath put in his own power". Then, He commanded them to be His witnesses, taking the message to Jerusalem, Judea, Samaria (which included the Gentiles) and the ends of the earth.

Yeshua exited earth with His mission as Saviour completed. The dual role of the Messiah, as promised in the Word, necessitated a second coming. Yeshua comes, at that time, to *physically sit on the throne of His earthly lineage, that of King David.* Herein lies the answer to the apostle's question, "Lord, wilt thou *at this time* restore again the kingdom to Israel?"[96] Restoration of the kingdom, with a physical king sitting on the throne of David, happens on Yeshua's return. That return the angels declared to the disciples with these words, "Ye men of Galilee, why stand ye gazing up into

---

[96] Acts 1:6

CHAPTER 12
His Weaponry of His Coming

heaven? this same Jesus, which is taken up from you into heaven, shall so come in like manner as ye have seen him go into heaven."[97]

In summary, the angel's message to Yoseph and Miriam indicated two purposes of Messiah's coming.[98] Likewise, Yeshua's words in the synagogue in Nazareth declared the same two purposes, defining them into two days:
- the acceptable day of YeHoVaH, (coming as Saviour) and
- the day of vengeance[99] (coming as the ruler with a rod of iron sitting on the throne of His Father, David[100]).

HIS WEAPONRY OF HIS COMING

God's message of salvation preached to all, as shown in the previous chapter, falls within the category of the acceptable day of YeHoVaH. That acceptable day continues, today, and applies until Yeshua's second coming, at which time, the day of vengeance begins. As to when that day of vengeance begins, the Bible does not

---

[97] Acts 1:11
[98] Which by the way, scripture verifies as Messiah is both Saviour and King!
[99] Isaiah 61:1-3 Luke 4:18-21
[100] Revelation 19:15

THE WARRIOR BRIDE
Advancing God's Kingdom Through Warfare

say anymore than it did with Yeshua's first coming as Saviour. However, just like YeHoVaH gave clues to that first coming through applicable prophetic words, so too, we find prophetic words applicable to His second coming, which allows YeHoVaH's people to know when the timeframe draws near.

This timeframe, the Bride, with eyes focused on her Betrothed, must consider important. Additionally, she must embrace the urgency of the message. While the exact day of vengeance, obviously won't arrive until its designated timeframe, God holds individuals, as well as rulers of nations, *in every generation* accountable for their actions.

This message of accountability, the Bride, preaches in love, in season and out of season, no matter the response. The Bride must preach this truth. She must, also, include the powerful message of the day of accountability as well as the day of vengeance!

Thus, as the Bride preaches the good news of the gospel, addressing the day of His coming within her message, she utilizes yet another weapon from her Beloved's arsenal.

CHAPTER 12
His Weaponry of His Coming

A FORGOTTEN ASPECT

When it comes to Yeshua's coming, many see Him arriving exactly as He left. However, many do not understand the second coming well enough to allow their impression of Him to shift from a servant to a warrior. While Yeshua returns, according to the specification of the angel, "in like manner as ye have seen him go into heaven"[101], He comes in a resurrected body, but not as a servant to suffer at the hands of wicked men. Rather, He comes as YeHoVaH, the great and powerful One in Whom He is One!

He comes as a mighty warrior.
to fulfill His God-ordained agenda,
which includes a relationship with
His Mighty Warrior Bride!

---

[101] Acts 1:11 b.

CONCLUSION OF SECTION 2, PART 2

In this section of the book, we focused on the second part of the Bride's Creed: *To Love Our Neighbour*. For the sake of brevity, we explained only a few weapons of warfare available to the Bride as she reaches out to help her neighbour:
- His Weaponry of His Gospel
- His Weaponry of His Coming

Of course, the Bride has access to more weaponry as she moves forward to advance the Kingdom of God on earth. Weapons such as His Name and His Word apply to this section, too. In addition, the Bride employs prayer, either one on one or corporately. Every biblical tool the Bride employs in preaching the gospel, including tongues, which brings a message to a nonbeliever,[102] works at making a difference. Whatever Biblical weaponry the Bride uses, she makes an impact on all who have ears to hear and a heart to perceive what the Spirit says, for indeed she works with Him:

---

[102] 1 Corinthians 14: 22 Wherefore tongues are for a sign, not to them that believe, but to them that believe not: but prophesying [serveth] not for them that believe not, but for them which believe.

CHAPTER 12
His Weaponry of His Coming

Mark 16:20
"And they went forth, and preached every where, the Lord working with [them], and confirming the word with signs following. Amen."

In leaving this part of the book, *(Section 2, Part 2, To Love Our Neighbour)*, recall the Bride's commitment to humankind. While she keeps her single eyed relationship with her Betrothed, she loves others with God's heart of love, desiring the best for them. That means, she willingly presents the gospel, paying the necessary price[103] in her effort to help humankind align with God and truth.

Additionally, she looks forward to seeing her Betrothed with His gazing smile of pleasure as she presents Him with the fruit of her labours. With all her heart, as the Bride comes face to face with Him, she rejoices! She fulfilled the Creed given to her: *to love God with all her heart, mind, soul and strength and she loved her neighbour as herself.*

---

[103] This cost is not just financial! It includes cost such as time, personal commitment, etc.

THE WARRIOR BRIDE
Advancing God's Kingdom Through Warfare

"And the Spirit and the Bride say, Come. And let him that heareth say, Come. And let him that is athirst come. And whosoever will, let him take the water of life freely."

Revelation 22:17

SECTION 2

THE BRIDE MOBILIZED

Part 3: To Love Ourselves

13

HIS WEAPONRY OF HIS PURITY

"Ye adulterers and adulteresses, know ye not that the friendship of the world is enmity with God? whosoever therefore will be a friend of the world is the enemy of God. Do ye think that the scripture saith in vain, The spirit that dwelleth in us lusteth to envy?

James 4:4-5

Looking at YeHoVaH and in analyzing His dealings with the people of God, as seen the in Bible, we see that His character in all circumstances shines forth as totally righteous and pure. As Yeshua came to earth He demonstrated that same character as He lived His life before His Father's eyes. Keeping in line with that same representation of the character of God, Yeshua looks for a Bride worthy of Him. Therefore, a

CHAPTER 13
His Weaponry of His Purity

Bride who makes herself ready, prepares to meet Him not by looking at an outward appearance, but rather by looking at her inner beauty, her character. In this manner, the Bride insures she lives her life in a manner pleasing to her Betrothed.

To do this, the Bride refers to the instructions which God gave her. In other words, she looks at the "mirror" of the Word to see her reflection. Thus, she sees where, *in her Beloved's eyes*, she reaches the goal set for her, as well as the ways in which she might fall short:

James 1:23-24

> 23 For if any be a hearer of the word, and not a doer, he is like unto a man beholding his natural face in a glass *(mirror):* 24 For he beholdeth himself, and goeth his way, and straightway forgetteth what manner of man he was.

Looking into the Bible, which is a mirror of the Word, the Bride recognizes her accurate appearance in God's eyes. Her desire to please her Betrothed takes over her and possesses her thoughts. Immediately, as she hears the Word, she quickly obeys, just as scripture admonishes:

THE WARRIOR BRIDE
Advancing God's Kingdom Through Warfare

James 1:21-22
> 21 Wherefore lay apart all filthiness and superfluity of naughtiness, and receive with meekness the engrafted word, which is able to save your souls. 22 But be ye doers of the word, and not hearers only, deceiving your own selves.

In loving her Betrothed, and her neighbour she realized the last part, which is to love herself. Her very heart of love towards Her Beloved, motivated her to love others. Likewise, that same love motivates her to love herself. She responds to all circumstances around her, not as her emotions or ideas dictate, but rather, she moves towards righteousness as the Word of God decrees. This, of course, takes discipline, however, it lies beyond the scope of human intellect. Living in such a manner falls into the category of living the crucified life:

Galatians 2:20
> 20 I am crucified with Christ: nevertheless, I live; yet not I, but Christ liveth in me: and the life which I now live in the flesh I live by the faith of the Son of God, who loved me, and gave himself for me.

CHAPTER 13
His Weaponry of His Purity

Living the crucified life, the Bride forsakes the pull of the flesh to welcome the life of the Spirit, thus, embracing a law made possible by the covenant in Yeshua's blood:

> Romans 8:1-4
> 1 [There is] therefore now no condemnation to them which are in Christ Jesus, who walk not after the flesh, but after the Spirit. 2 For the law of the Spirit of life in Christ Jesus hath made me free from the law of sin and death. 3 For what the law could not do, in that it was weak through the flesh, God sending his own Son in the likeness of sinful flesh, and for sin, condemned sin in the flesh: 4 That the righteousness of the law might be fulfilled in us, who walk not after the flesh, but after the Spirit.

To completely live the crucified life, the Bride learns to forsake the flesh and walk in the law of the Spirit. This is a shift to partake of a greater law which God gave humankind, through Yeshua: *The Law of the Spirit of Life*. This Law employs the resurrection power of Yeshua. Thus, as the Bride walks by the Spirit, she fulfills the desires of God, completing the royal law[104], which is the Bride's Creed:

> James 2:8
> 8 ¶ If ye fulfil the royal law according to the scripture, Thou shalt love thy neighbour as thyself, ye do well:

To set this scripture within its proper light, we see James refers to the topic of behaviour which expresses partiality. James addresses the importance of not judging others, or moving in such a manner as to gain favour with one group, while ignoring another:

> James 2:1-7
> 1 ¶ My brethren, have not the faith of our Lord Jesus Christ, [the Lord] of glory, with respect of persons. 2 For if there come unto your assembly a man with a gold ring, in goodly apparel, and there come in also a poor man in vile raiment; 3 And ye have respect to him that weareth the gay clothing, and say unto him, Sit thou here in

---

[104] The Royal Law is to love God with all your heart, mind, soul and strength and your neighbour as yourself.

CHAPTER 13
His Weaponry of His Purity

a good place; and say to the poor, Stand thou there, or sit here under my footstool: 4 Are ye not then partial in yourselves, and are become judges of evil thoughts? 5 Hearken, my beloved brethren, Hath not God chosen the poor of this world rich in faith, and heirs of the kingdom which he hath promised to them that love him? 6 But ye have despised the poor. Do not rich men oppress you, and draw you before the judgment seats? 7 Do not they blaspheme that worthy name by the which ye are called?

No matter the person's social status, influence or financial background, race, or colour each person deserves the same love, respect and measure of grace as the other. In caring for others, the Bride remembers this equality, while at the same time, looks at her own behaviour, looking for her own errors where she might fail, and when she finds things, then, she employs that same grace and mercy to herself as she expresses to others.

Thus, in summary, the Bride loves her Betrothed, she loves her neighbour forgiving them on behalf of her Betrothed, but also forgiving herself for any areas where she falls short.

Since she lives in the light and not in the dark, she exposes what goes wrong, in all things, *including areas where she falls short*. When she discovers something unacceptable to her Beloved, she looks to God for His provision:

1 John 1:8 -2:6
> 8 ¶ If we say that we have no sin, we deceive ourselves, and the truth is not in us. 9 If we confess our sins, he is faithful and just to forgive us [our] sins, and to cleanse us from all unrighteousness. 10 If we say that we have not sinned, we make him a liar, and his word is not in us.
>
> 2:1 ¶ My little children, these things write I unto you, that ye sin not. And if any man sin, we have an advocate with the Father, Jesus Christ the righteous: 2 And he is the propitiation for our sins: and not for ours only, but also for [the sins of] the whole world. 3 ¶ And hereby we do know that we know him if we keep his commandments. 4 He that saith, I know him, and keepeth not his commandments,

CHAPTER 13
His Weaponry of His Purity

is a liar, and the truth is not in him. 5 But whoso keepeth his word, in him verily is the love of God perfected: hereby know we that we are in him. 6 He that saith he abideth in him ought himself also so to walk, even as he walked.

Living in the honest light of the truth, to love oneself means looking at God's true reality. Since individual believers make up the Bride, and as such express their own free will, sin happens after salvation. Perhaps, not intentional sin, but nevertheless, reality teaches us that people fall short of their goal of walking in the Spirit. Yet, as the Bride loves herself, she does not hide any sin! Rather, she exposes it! She brings it before the One to Whom she serves. In doing so, she implements His provision for sin after salvation:

1 John 2:1-2

> 1 ¶ My little children, these things write I unto you, that ye sin not. And if any man sin, we have an advocate with the Father, Jesus Christ the righteous: 2 And he is the propitiation for our sins: and not for ours only, but also for [the sins of] the whole world.

In this manner of self-love, we recognize the provision God has for us when we fail. Also, we see the need to walk away from the things which draw us into sin. In those ways, we do not conform to the World and all that is in it, rather, *we conform to the Word and all that is in it!*

Paul, the Apostle, put it this way in Romans 12:1-2

"1 ¶ I beseech you therefore, brethren, by the mercies of God, that ye present your bodies a living sacrifice, holy, acceptable unto God, [which is] your reasonable service. 2 And be not conformed to this world: but be ye transformed by the renewing of your mind, that ye may prove what [is] that good, and acceptable, and perfect, will of God.

HIS WEAPONRY OF HIS PURITY

In loving oneself, therefore, each believer lives out their life before the face of YeHoVaH, conforming to the Word and its requirements. As believers obey this scripture, their mind enjoys a transformation, renewed to align with the Word of God, which leads into all righteousness, holiness and purity. Thus,

CHAPTER 13
His Weaponry of His Purity

believers live out and prove that which is the good, acceptable and perfect will of God.

Each believer living to fulfill God's Word, as a small part of the whole, then, aims for a pure heart as God desires, embracing completely, the mindsets of God. Thus, as more of the body walks in the light, living in purity before His Face, the whole becomes stronger by the strengthening of the one individual.

With regards to the Body of Messiah, God requires that no one despise any part of the Body of Messiah, but rather gives mercy, looking at the Body of Messiah as God does:

Romans 12:3-5
> 3 For I say, through the grace given unto me, to every man that is among you, not to think [of himself] more highly than he ought to think; but to think soberly, according as God hath dealt to every man the measure of faith. 4 For as we have many members in one body, and all members have not the same office: 5 So we, [being] many, are one body in Christ, and everyone members one of another.

Thus, the Bride, walking within the mindset of her Beloved, recognizes the need for her oneness with Him, for this righteousness of God requires and aims to walk in a oneness with her fellow members, supporting them in their Divine tasks. She encourages all to fulfill the overall will of God:

> Romans 12:6-8
> 6 Having then gifts differing according to the grace that is given to us, whether prophecy, [let us prophesy] according to the proportion of faith; 7 Or ministry, [let us wait] on [our] ministering: or he that teacheth, on teaching; 8 Or he that exhorteth, on exhortation: he that giveth, [let him do it] with simplicity; he that ruleth, with diligence; he that sheweth mercy, with cheerfulness.

Respecting individual giftings and their part in bringing about the whole, believers learn to respect and love one another.

> Romans 12:9-15
> 9 [Let] love be without dissimulation. Abhor that which is evil; cleave to that which is good. 10 [Be] kindly affectioned

CHAPTER 13
His Weaponry of His Purity

one to another with brotherly love; in honour preferring one another; 11 Not slothful in business; fervent in spirit; serving the Lord; 12 Rejoicing in hope; patient in tribulation; continuing instant in prayer; 13 Distributing to the necessity of saints; given to hospitality. 14 Bless them which persecute you: bless, and curse not. 15 Rejoice with them that do rejoice, and weep with them that weep.

Every believer honouring the Word of God and expressing one to another, builds up the body as they embrace the same mindset as described by the Word.

Romans 12:16-18
16 [Be] of the same mind one toward another. Mind not high things but condescend to men of low estate. Be not wise in your own conceits. 17 Recompense to no man evil for evil. Provide things honest in the sight of all men. 18 If it be possible, as much as lieth in you, live peaceably with all men

As the Bride lives out the Word of God, she fulfills the Royal Law, which includes love towards herself, namely, *her own individual members*. She sees no believer as competition, nor a threat to any agenda. She does not despise them for their differences or various individual giftings but rather, sees them as fulfilling their part in the overall plan of God. Of course, the Bride never overlooks nor excuses sin, but with a love and discernment of the true source of sin, exposes that sin. In doing so, she realizes the value of confronting sin with the truth, and walks before YeHoVaH in a way that honours Him and others:

He hath shewed thee, O man, what [is] good; and what doth YeHoVaH require of thee, but to do justly, and to love mercy, and to walk humbly with thy God?

Micah 6:8

14

HIS WEAPONRY OF HIS SEASONS

I must work the works of him that sent me, while it is day: the night cometh, when no man can work.

John 9:4

Prior to the 1800's, before the dawn of artificial lights, once night arrived, labours ceased. Man rested. In the poorer segments of society, nighttime hours passed by with sleep. For those wealthier members of society, sleep often took second place, giving way to evening activities of another sort. To light these festivities, they used torches to provide light. However, any ability to work, other than servants serving their masters, they suspended till daylight. Only then, normal business resumed. This way of life continued until the dawning of the light bulb.

CHAPTER 14
His Weaponry of His Season

As we reflect on biblical passages, such as found in John 9:2-5, we need to remember the way in which man lived after dark in ancient days, as understanding the way they lived sheds some light[105] upon the meaning of this verse:

John 9:2-5
"2 And his disciples asked him, saying, Master, who did sin, this man, or his parents, that he was born blind? 3 Jesus answered, Neither hath this man sinned, nor his parents: but that the works of God should be made manifest in him. 4 I must work the works of him that sent me, while it is day: the night cometh, when no man can work. 5 As long as I am in the world, I am the light of the world."

Yeshua relayed a message to His disciples about the nighttime, which in His time, saw most people sleeping, not working. Considering the common knowledge of His time when night arrived, work ceased. Thus, Yeshua said *"I must work the works of him that sent me, while it is day: the night cometh, when no man can work."*[106]

---

[105] No pun intended.
[106] John 9:4

THE WARRIOR BRIDE
Advancing God's Kingdom Through Warfare

Here we have two important comments:

1. Work while it is day.
2. When nighttime comes, no man works.

Earlier, before giving this message, Yeshua passed by a man born blind from birth. His disciples asked Him to explain the cause of this blindness. "Did this man sin or his parents?"[107] Neither, Yeshua clarified. This blindness came that works of God would be manifest. Thus, Yeshua prepared to heal the man. He made clay with his spital, put it on the blind man's eyes, then sent him away to wash his eyes in the pool of Siloam[108]. After following Yeshua's instructions, the blind man went his way with 100% restored vision.

To understand this event, we must realize that the Jews believed that the Messiah would lead Israel to victory over their enemies, thus ruling a kingdom whose power would exceed the other nations around them. Thus, Israel's supremacy as a world power would rise again as in the days of King David. To recognize this Messiah, God would give them signs, among

---
[107] John 9:2
[108] John 9:6-7

CHAPTER 14
His Weaponry of His Season

them this one: *the Messiah would heal a man born blind.*

As Yeshua healed the man born blind, His very action stirred the leaders in Israel as that healing pointed a strong finger in Yeshua's favour to show Him as Messiah. Keeping that thought in mind, read these words of Yeshua, again:

> John 9:4-5
> 4 I must work the works of him that sent me, while it is day: the night cometh, when no man can work. 5 As long as I am in the world, I am the light of the world.

Primarily, upon reading these words, "I am the Light of the world", believers connect this miracle with the darkness associated with blindness, such as that experienced by the man born blind, however, considering Yeshua's earlier comment in verse 4, "I must work the works of him that sent me, while it is day", we have a deeper meaning here.

First, we know that Yeshua came to save His people from their sins. That fact is clear as the angel spoke His name to Joseph:

THE WARRIOR BRIDE
Advancing God's Kingdom Through Warfare

Matthew 1:21
   21 And she shall bring forth a son, and thou shalt call his name JESUS: for he shall save his people from their sins.

As Yeshua made clay from His spital, He began the miracle to do the impossible, yet He provided the important sign that indicated their Messiah in their midst. Yeshua did the works, ones which Israel's leaders and people saw. It was the day of their Redemption, the day of their Messiah, however, the night drew near. That time, Yeshua said, no man can work.

To what night did He refer?

Yeshua referred to the time when the season changed from the day of acceptability to the day of vengeance. At that time, night arrives in the world. However, as long as it is day, His light shines bright for all to see.

Dear Reader, today, Yeshua's Bride lives within the day of acceptability. It is DAY TIME! As a part of the Body of Messiah, each believer must be about the business of the Kingdom of God, especially as the night approaches. Soon the Bridegroom, Yeshua, sounds the trumpet call to

CHAPTER 14
His Weaponry of His Season

announce His coming for the Bride! Soon the day of the Wedding feast, planned since before the world began, takes place! We must work while it is still daylight to help others into the kingdom of God!

DAYS OF NOAH

To understand that time prior to His coming Yeshua told us:

> Matthew 24:36-39
> "36 But of that day and hour knoweth no [man], no, not the angels of heaven, but my Father only. 37 But as the days of Noe [were], so shall also the coming of the Son of man be. 38 For as in the days that were before the flood they were eating and drinking, marrying and giving in marriage, until the day that Noe entered into the ark, 39 And knew not until the flood came, and took them all away; so, shall also the coming of the Son of man be."

People, in the days prior to the flood, went about doing their own business. According to scripture, their business included doing their own thing to the extent, their evil hearts sought satisfaction in violence:

THE WARRIOR BRIDE
Advancing God's Kingdom Through Warfare

Genesis 6:11-12

11 ¶ The earth also was corrupt before God, and the earth was filled with violence. 12 And God looked upon the earth, and behold, it was corrupt; for all flesh had corrupted his way upon the earth.

Man's heart, before the flood, thought only of violence. None sought YeHoVaH, nor loved their neighbour, except for Noah and certain members of his household. Obviously, humankind reached its point of total corruption, which in no way desired repentance. Noah's preaching did not change them! Constantly, they resisted the Holy Spirit, Who, at one point, gives up pleading with man:

Genesis 6:3

3 And the LORD said, My spirit shall not always strive with man, for that he also [is] flesh: yet his days shall be an hundred and twenty years.

When humankind's heart reaches a certain point of corruption, he refuses repentance. When that happens, the Holy Spirit no longer seeks to convict of sin, those who refuse to yield to Him. Thus, as in Noah's time, God had no

CHAPTER 14
His Weaponry of His Season

choice but to destroy that world. However, He redeemed a righteous man and his family.

Similarly, before the Son of Man returns for His Bride, the earth's inhabitants, will mostly refuse God's call to repentance. They will reject His Spirit's conviction to forsake unrighteousness and seek righteousness. The bottom line: *these people, deeply immersed in sin, will retain their own ways and in no wise, give access to the Spirit of God to help them either through correction, repentance or redemption.* These people totally align with the works of darkness, refusing any aspect of the light to expose their wicked ways, and thus, eternal darkness becomes their reward, for that is what they sought.

In this horrible state the world operated, not even touched by Noah's preaching. Such a season comes again, before the Son of Man returns.

HIS WEAPONRY OF HIS SEASON
Warned of this season coming, when it is so dark no man worketh but rather the day of vengeance arrives, the Bride sheds her light of truth wherever she goes. While some may seek to measure the success of the Bride by looking

at the measure of fruit reaped, that measuring stick fails in seasons when humankind refuses to repent. A better measuring stick, as mentioned in an earlier chapter, is not the reception of the gospel message, but its constant proclamation.

As the Bride thinks about her Beloved and prepares to meet Him, she must employ every effort to reap the harvest. She may, in certain harvest seasons of abundance, rejoice, however, the Bride, *especially as the night draws near*, must keep her eyes focused on her Beloved. To Him she must look, more and more until the day heaven parts and He returns.

In this season, as the Bride lives out the last days of the acceptable year of YeHoVaH, she remembers the season of the coming night when no one works.

CONCLUSION OF SECTION 3, PART 3

Like her Beloved, the Bride does the work assigned to her while it is day. She loves herself, her own members of the Body, and unites with them to bring about the common goal of the Kingdom of God. She, also, understands that

CHAPTER 14
His Weaponry of His Season

light she sheds, knowing that it will draw some souls into the Kingdom, and thus, at those times, she'll see a great harvest. However, there will be times when the inhabitants of the earth seek to destroy her light and put it out. Those days of persecution do come, yet she must walk through with as much grace and mercy as she does in times of great harvest. Outside influences must never affect her agenda. For her Beloved, the Bride works before night falls, remembering these words of the Psalmist:

Psalm 109:4
4 For my love they are my adversaries: but I give myself unto prayer.

FINAL COMMENTS

Throughout this book, you've read about the various weapons of warfare the Bride incorporates to win lost souls. That implementation of her Beloved's weaponry, make up the warrior Bride. In reality, she has but one purpose, but one goal: **to win lost souls**. Thus, as the Bride's structure of individual believers unite for that common goal, she functions as one in God's eyes.

THE WARRIOR BRIDE
Advancing God's Kingdom Through Warfare

To YeHoVaH, the Bride emulates His character, operating as the Light of the World, shining into the darkness like a beacon to call the lost home. To the world, the Bride brings love, mercy, and redemption, in season and out of season[109]. To herself, the Bride looks with love and mercy upon all her members supporting them as they unite for the common good.

No matter where the Bride goes, no matter the season in which she lives, the Bride exposes, reveals and brings God's solution to that which displeases Him in an effort to push back that which causes darkness to invade people's lives. She exposes sin, which include those of her own individual members, as well as those of others living outside the Body of Messiah. Again, the goal is for salvation, deliverance and healing, to bring about a better thing than the result of sin, which, according to God's Word, brings forth death:

Romans 6:23

---

[109] When people hear the gospel and either tolerate, allow or receive those preaching it (in season); or when they refuse to hear it and persecute those who speak it (out of season).

CHAPTER 14
His Weaponry of His Season

23 For the wages of sin [is] death; but the gift of God [is] eternal life through Jesus Christ our Lord.

While the world and its philosophies, which hold hands with ha satan, does not like to think its ways fall into the category of sin, the fact remains that God says so. People, unfortunately, caught in the deception and lies of ha satan, end up calling good evil and evil good.[110] Thus, their view of God, His Laws, and those who follow them becomes out of alignment with the Light of Heaven and stand in agreement with ha satan.

To the people, captives of darkness, the Word of God, nevertheless, must come! For such Yeshua died! Therefore, the extended and loving arms of the Bride reaches out to help them, no matter the results, or even when persecuted for bringing the gospel message.

PERSONAL APPLICATION

In 1 Corinthians Chapter 12, Paul, the Apostle, addresses the importance of each member of the Bride of Messiah by comparing the wholeness of the Bride to the individual members of a

---

[110] Isaiah 5:20

person's body. He highlights the importance of each member of a person's body and how it all functions together, then compares it to the overall function to the Body of Messiah, as each member works together to complete their own, unique role, yet remain in unity with one another focusing on the same goal.

Paul knew the importance of the Bride grasping and accepting her individual roles for the corporate goal of the Kingdom of God. Naturally, each individual believer, which makes up the corporate Bride, has a choice: to accept or refuse their own individual role. However, those whose heart aligns with truth, do obey the Holy Spirit's leading. Thus, out of that oneness with the Spirit comes the fulfillment of YeHoVaH's plan for the Bride.

Dear reader, *your heart is tender to the truth, or else you would not be interested in studying the Bible; thus, you will do your own unique role within the Body of Messiah by yielding to the Holy Spirit.* While your part in your eyes, may seem small, insignificant, or perhaps even unimportant, God's wisdom teaches in the Word that we do not compare our role to that of another. Therefore, dear reader, see yourself and your

CHAPTER 14
His Weaponry of His Season

role as part of the whole, fulfilling your assigned responsibility, bit by bit, step by step. See that role as God's best for your life, for the Bride, and for the Kingdom of God.

Remember, God's Kingdom advances, dear one, as you, as one of its members, employ the weaponry of God to see captives set free! Swing well the sword of the Spirit (the Word of God), stand for righteousness in your generation, wearing your spiritual armour. Fulfill your entire role in the functioning body of Messiah on the earth. Employ His Weaponry in your life for yourself, emulating His character, and moving as the Spirit leads. On His behalf, touch the lives of others: *On one hand deter ha satan from his goals and on the other hand, reach out your Beloved's Hand of love with the gospel to affect the world around you.* This is the dual role of the Bride! This is the way to advance the Kingdom of God.

"Fight the good fight of faith, lay hold on eternal life, whereunto thou art also called, and hast professed a good profession before many witnesses."

1 Timothy 6:12

THE WARRIOR BRIDE
Advancing God's Kingdom Through Warfare

Do not weary of the battle for in the end, it reaps a great reward. Walk out your faith in fear and trembling, dear one, remembering every aspect of your faith, ***including that of the Warrior Bride!***

"Finally, my brethren, be strong in the Lord, and in the power of his might. Put on the whole armour of God, that ye may be able to stand against the wiles of the devil."
Ephesians 6:10-11

FINAL REFLECTION

In beginning this book, you read of an interesting vision, where God portrayed the Bride of Messiah as a beautiful Bride, praising Him and moving along in power, radically changing the world around her. Then, you saw a portrayal of eyes of fire as the Bride encountered spiritual opponents who desire to deter humankind from an eternal destiny with God. In subsequent chapters, you read about the dual role of the Bride, which encompasses love to God, man and self, and a pure, holy and wholesome approach to dealing with the forces of darkness.

CHAPTER 14
His Weaponry of His Season

Now, whenever you think about God coming for His Bride, reflect upon the dual role of the Bride. Recognize this as her God-given role from heaven. See the Bride as beautiful in every way: *inside* (with the glory of God dwelling therein), and *outside* (with the love of God flowing like an endless river). Then, see the eyes of her Betrothed glistening with joy as He breaks through the heavens and brings His Beloved to His Side. Listen as He says to her, *(of whom you are a part)*, "Well done". Truly, dear reader, is this not the goal, the end for which we live?

APPENDIX

A NAME TO HONOUR

YeHoVaH[111]

"So will I make my holy name known in the midst of my people Israel; and I will not let them pollute my holy name any more: and the heathen shall know that I am YeHoVaH, the Holy One in Israel."

Ezekiel 39:7

f, today, someone asked you to tell them the name of your earthly father, without hesitation Iyou would declare it. If, for some reason, you did not know your earthly father, you would also say so, and perhaps give some explanation as to why you don't know his name. So, if today, you are asked to relate the name of your

---

[111] Based on information given by Michael Rood, partly from his work entitled, The Chronological Bible, and partly from his numerous YouTube videos. For more information see his website and/or page 28 of the Chronological Bible.

heavenly Father would you do so with ease, or would you draw a blank?

Most of Christendom, today, is totally ignorant as to the name of the Father, as well as the way it is pronounced. As the author of this book on heaven, I'd like to join the ranks of those who wish to relate that name to the world. After all, when we stand before the Father on the day, we give an account for our deeds in this body, it would be a good thing to know Him, His Name and how it is pronounced!

Did you know that the name of the Father appears at least 6,828 times in the Hebrew scriptures? It is there written as four specific Hebrew letters. They are as follows:

> י Pronounced yode, or yod
> ה Pronounced as hey
> ו Pronounced as Vav
> ה Pronounced as hey

For centuries, whenever the Jews come across these 4 letters they simply say, Adonai, or Ha Shem (meaning the name). They refuse to pronounce the name for several reasons, some of which we will look at momentarily. For now, let's look at whether their tradition affected Christianity. That can be easily done by looking at our Bibles to see if the 4-letter name of the Father is clearly presented or substituted. A quick look reveals that in the KJV Bible, as well as in many other popular versions, the 4-letter name is presented to readers as a 4-letter English word, "LORD". [112] Whether intentional or not, Christendom has followed the ancient tradition of the Jews.

THE ANCIENT TRADITION OF THE JEWS
In early second century times[113] Rabbis hid the pronunciation of the holy name of God. They did this by omitting the vowel pointings, which are necessary to make the name pronounceable. Hence, as they carefully wrote the scriptures, their omittance of the vowel pointings made the name unpronounceable. Historians believe there were two reasons why they did this:

i. According to Josephus, Rome, under the rule of Domitian, 81 to 96 CE, put to

---

[112] At times, in certain places, some translators wrote the Hebrew name of YeHoVaH as "GOD" rather than "LORD".
[113] Or according to other authorities, much further back in time.

death anyone using the name of the Jewish or Christian God.

ii. It is also believed, Rabbis borrowed a tradition from pagans, whereby the name of their god was considered too holy to mention, so they called him "Baal" meaning Lord. The Jews adopted this practice and most still practice it today, even some Messianic Jews!

THEIR TRADITION CONTINUES

Bible translators followed their tradition for reasons which are not presently understood. Possibly, it may have occurred because the pronunciation of the name was totally forgotten, or totally hidden by those who knew[114]. Whatever the reason, following this tradition made the readers of Bibles, who are mostly believers, continue in this tradition. The problem here is not just the tradition, but the bottom line of the tradition is this:

Does that tradition offend the Heavenly Father?

If indeed its origin was Baal worship, then we can give a resounding Amen to the fact it

---

[114] According to some, the Jews secretly knew the name.

offends God. In addition, as we look at scripture, we see the Almighty was not pleased with this, for His Heart is for all to be saved, including the Gentiles. How can they be saved if they don't know the name upon which to call? Scripture [115] clearly states that in the end times, His name would be known so that the Gentiles can call upon it and be saved. Obviously, for that to happen, the name of יְהֹוָה must be made known.

AN HISTORIC DISCOVERY
Today, some Hebrew scholars[116] have searched the world over for Hebrew manuscripts. In doing so, they have found many Hebrew documents which contain the full name with vowels and therefore the pronunciation of the name. These scholars may differ slightly in pronunciation, but nevertheless, they are making the name of YeHoVaH known today.

---

[115] Jeremiah 16:1-21

[116] Nehemiah Gordon was the Hebrew scholar who found the name of the Father, with all vowel pointings, and through his efforts and those of others, that name with vowels pointings has been found in over 2000 manuscripts.

A DELIGHTFUL SIDE NOTE:

In looking at the Hebrew root of the name of the Father, which is pronounced *Ya-Ho* **Vah'**, and looking at another scripture, we see something amazing about our Saviour. In speaking of the Prophet, the one the Father would send to Him we all must listen and obey, YeHoVaH said that His name would be in the name of the Prophet.

Exodus 23:21 "Beware of him, and obey his voice, provoke him not; for he will not pardon your transgressions[117]: *for my name [is] in him.*"

Our Saviour's name, as given by the angel was "Yehoshua".

י	Pronounced yode or yod
ה	Pronounced hey
ו	Pronounced vav
ש	Pronounced shin
ע	Pronounced ayin

The name of the Father is in the name of the Son! The first three letters of YeHoVaH show it! (Yod, Heh, Vav). Is it so amazing that the name

---

[117] Please keep in mind that Yeshua bore the punishment for your sins. Your sins were not pardoned, they were atoned!

of our Father is in the true name of the One YeHoVaH sent to redeem us!

HONOUR THE FATHER'S NAME

Throughout this book, and all subsequent books, as well as all accompanying audios and PowerPoints, it is the author's intention to widely use, proclaim and continually pronounce the name of the Father. Indeed, this breaks with tradition, but thus far as we've shared the news of the Father's name, reception has been excellent.

NAME CHALLENGE:

Since, as of this reading, you are no longer ignorant of your heavenly Father's name, please join the unofficial network of proclaimers of the Father's name and shout it to the house tops.

Romans 10: 12-15

12 ¶ For there is no difference between the Jew and the Greek: for the same Lord over all is rich unto all that call upon him. 13 For whosoever shall call upon the name of YeHoVaH shall be saved. 14 How then shall they call on him in whom they have not believed? and how shall they believe in him of whom they have not heard? and how shall they hear without a preacher?

15 And how shall they preach, except they be sent? as it is written, How beautiful are the feet of them that preach the gospel of peace and bring glad tidings of good things!

SALVATION'S MESSAGE

Yeshua, when walking on earth, said this:

John 3:14-18wor
14 And as Moses lifted up the serpent in the wilderness, even so must the Son of man be lifted up: 15 That whosoever believeth in him should not perish but have eternal life. 16 For God so loved the world, that he gave his only begotten Son, that whosoever believeth in him should not perish, but have everlasting life. 17 For God sent not his Son into the world to condemn the world; but that the world through him might be saved. 18 He that believeth on him is not condemned: but he that believeth not is condemned already, because he hath not believed in the name of the only begotten Son of God.

During the time of Moses, the children of Israel, in the wilderness, rebelled against God, at which time poisonous serpents infiltrated the camp, killing many of the people. After seeking YeHoVaH for a solution to the problem, Moses followed

God's instructions and made a bronze serpent fashioned and erected it on a pole in sight of the people. Whosoever wanted to live, must acknowledge their rebellion against YeHoVaH, and in doing so, look upon the erected pole and bronze serpent, to YeHoVaH, who gave them life in place of death, then they would live.

Yeshua said, just as Moses erected that bronze serpent in the wilderness, He would be lifted up. This referred to the event, in the future, of Yeshua's crucifixion. During the time when the serpent hung on that pole, whosoever wanted to live and not die from the serpent's bite must acknowledge their rebellion, their sin against YeHoVaH. Likewise, for those who wish to live eternally, they must look upon the cross of the crucified One, to YeHoVaH, who provided life for them. This was an act of love for all humankind, necessary because man is born from Adam, and thus is born with an inherent sin. Secondly, man sins. The consequence of sin is death, and eternal death, wherein man will spend an eternity in darkness, away from YeHoVaH. Unfortunately, there is nothing humanly possible to reverse those consequences. Even if a person had made a genuine decision never to sin again, and for some reason they succeeded, all their good deeds and good living would not erase the penalty of eternal death.

There is only *one way* for Eternal Life to touch a person's life. That is the way Yeshua explained to His listeners:
through the works of God on the cross of Calvary.

Salvation comes by understanding these facts:
1. Yeshua, being the Son of God and the fulfillment of the scriptures, never sinned
2. YeHoVaH, on behalf of every human being on the earth, chose to make Yeshua become as sin, in His Eyes, so that Yeshua might pay the penalty for sin, for all of humanity.
3. Yeshua paid that penalty. He died on the cross and was buried in a tomb.
4. Three days later, He rose again, appearing to His disciples, to show them the reality of His resurrection, to show

them God vindicated Him and made Him both Lord and Messiah.
5. Yeshua could not stay in the tomb, because "death" comes to all who sin, but since Yeshua never sinned, therefore, death could not hold Him in the grave.
6. All those who come to Yeshua, to receive Him as their Saviour, receive liberty from sin and from its horrible consequence, eternal death.
7. They enter YeHoVaH's kingdom and receive eternal life, as well as another gift: **The Righteousness of Messiah.** After salvation, when YeHoVaH looks upon a believer in Messiah, He sees Yeshua's perfect life and sees a redeemed believer, set aside for YeHoVaH. Since salvation has taken place in the believer, the Holy Spirit dwells within them.
8. All it takes to receive salvation from YeHoVaH is receiving His Messiah, fully repenting from sinning against God. [118] YeHoVaH even gives the believer the faith to receive His gift of Salvation!

The Apostle Paul put it this way:

---

[118] And against man. When a person steals, etc. they sin against both God and man,

Ephesians 2:8
"For by grace are ye saved through faith; and that not of yourselves: it is the gift of God"

When you pray the following prayer, realize it is written here to get you started in your walk with YeHoVaH. To be truly saved, you make a life's commitment! There is not just a one-time prayer and you're done! From this moment on, seek YeHoVaH for His help in all things, including to follow through with your commitment until the very end!

SINNER'S PRAYER & LIFETIME COMMITMENT

Heavenly, Father:

I acknowledge before You, Lord, that I am a sinner. I understand sin's punishment is a life without You, for all eternity. Thank You for sending Yeshua to the earth, as the Messiah. I understand now that He died in my place, to take my punishment for my sins. I believe You raised Yeshua from the dead, and now that I've I accept Him as my personal Saviour, my old life dies, and my new life begins.

I humbly ask You, Lord, to forgive me of my sins, and as of this moment, I receive Yeshua as my Mashiach. I open my heart to receive the works of the cross that You provided for me through Yeshua, and with Your help, I will walk away from my sin, turning my back upon my own will and ways. I will now live my life seeking to obey Your Word and Your will. Help me to live, from this point onward, in a manner pleasing to You.

Amen

*****

If you prayed that prayer, please be sure you tell someone. Remember that a person believes with the heart unto righteousness and confesses with their mouth unto salvation, as spoken about in Romans 10:10.

> 10 For with the heart man believeth unto righteousness; and with the mouth confession is made unto salvation

One more thing:

Remember, this gospel message comes with power. When you hear it, the kingdom of God draws near to you. When you repent of your sins and receive Salvation, the kingdom of God moves within. You can't see it, feel it or tell it from an outward observing. It is accepted, received and lived out by faith!

Seek out other believers in Messiah and may God bless you richly as you live your live, now, completely for Him!

Other Books by This Author

An Arsenal of Powerful Prayers [119]
  Scriptural Prayers to Move Mountains,
Arising Incense
  A Believer's Priesthood
Candidate for A Miracle
  Wisdom from the miracles of Yeshua
Foundations of Revival
  Biblical Evidence for Revival
His Reflection
  What God longs to see in His People
Heaven's Greater Government
  Behind the Scenes of Earth's Events
In The Name of Yehovah We Set Up Our Banners
  Biblical use of banners
It's All About Heaven
  As Pictured in Scripture
Kingdom Keys for Kingdom Kids
  Walking in Kingdom Power
Molded for the Miraculous
  Why God made You
Releasing the Impossible
  The Limitless Power of Intercession
  Volume 1: Intercessions from the Author's life

---

[119] *This is a book of written prayers of various topics to help believers live a stronger, active faith. No workbook.*

Volume 2: Intercessions from Bibical Characters
Salvation Depicted in a Meal [120]
Passover Hagaddah
The Jeremiah Generation
God's Response to Injustice
The Warrior Bride-
God's Kingdom Advancing through Spiritual Warfare
Thy Kingdom Come
Entering God's Rest in Prayer
Watching, Waiting & Warning
Obeying Yeshua's Command to Watch & Pray
When Nations Rumble
A Study of the Book of Amos
Worship in Spirit and In Truth [121]
The Tabernacle of David - Past, Present & Future

---

[120] *Haggadah (Guide) for a Christian Passover. No Workbook.*
[121] *Good sister book to "In the Name of YeHoVaH we set up our banners".*

ABOUT THE KING JAMES VERSION

Scriptures quoted in this book *originate* from the KJV **public domain version** of the Bible, which means, no copyright exists on this version of the scripture. While some find this translation outdated, Jeanne, trained in the KJV still finds this version helpful, and uses it in all her books[122].

In using KJV, however, it is good to remember the following:

- Some words in the KJV have changed meaning over the centuries. To understand such words, look up the root word in its original language. In doing so, the meaning stands out. For example. KJV uses the word "conversation" however, in its original language it means moral character, or behaviour.
- When KJV spoke of humanity, they said, "man". When you read that word, or hear others speak about the scriptures using the term, "man", know it refers to all humankind, not a specific gender.

---

[122] In later manuscripts, the author updated the more archaic words in the KJV such as wouldest or couldest.

Due to tradition, the name of the Father, YeHoVaH appears as LORD, or at times as Jehovah. However, in all Jeanne's manuscripts, YeHoVaH's name replaces the term LORD. To learn more read "A Name to Honour", located in this Appendix section.

SCRIPTURE INDEX

1

1 Chronicles 16:23-29 93
1 Corinthians 12:13 126
1 Corinthians 14: 22 197
1 Corinthians 15:52-57 . 153
1 John 1:8 -2:6 209
1 John 2:1-2 210
1 Samuel 13:14 80
1 Samuel 15:19-23 77
1 Samuel 15:21 77
1 Samuel 16:17-19 79
1 Samuel 9: 78
1 Samuel 9:2 76
1 Timothy 6:12 230

2

2 Chronicles 17:3-5 83
2 Chronicles 20:14-17 84
2 Chronicles 20:18-21 86
2 Chronicles 20:22-26 87
2 Corinthians 10:1-6 61
2 Corinthians 10:4 ...59, 164
2 Corinthians 4:3-7 171
2 Thessalonians 2:13-15 . 45
2 Timothy 2:15 111
2 Timothy 4:1-2 170

A

Acts 1: 193
Acts 1:1 194
Acts 1:6-11 191
Acts 13:10-11 177

Acts 13:5-12 175
Acts 13:9-11 178
Acts 16:16-18 142
Acts 16:19-24 143
Acts 16:25 -27 144
Acts 16:28-34 145
Acts 9:8 180

D

Daniel 4: 17 149
Deuteronomy 6: 5 81
Deuteronomy 6:4 ......40, 42

E

Ecclesiastes 7:1 94
Ephesians 1:15-23 136
Ephesians 2:4-10 139
Ephesians 2:8 247
Ephesians 6:10-11 231
Ephesians 6:12 173
Exodus 17 124
Exodus 19:5-6 27
Exodus 23:21 240
Exodus 34:28 34
Ezekiel 39:7 235

G

Galatians 2:20 205
Genesis 1:28 151
Genesis 1:3-5 107
Genesis 1:6-8 108
Genesis 1:9-10 108
Genesis 11:24 49

Genesis 11:26 49
Genesis 15:2 49
Genesis 24:13-14 50
Genesis 24:17-20 50
Genesis 24:1-8 49
Genesis 24:21-2 51
Genesis 24:34b to 49 52
Genesis 24:59-61- 52
Genesis 24:62-6 53
Genesis 24:67 54
Genesis 6:3 223

H

Hebrews 1:1-4 152
Hebrews 11:13-16 ... 13, 161
Hebrews 11 14
Hebrews 4:12 109

I

Isaiah 11:1-5 129
Isaiah 40:17 158
Isaiah 40:31 133
Isaiah 45:1-3 20
Isaiah 45:17 102
Isaiah 54:4-5 23
Isaiah 61:1-3 187
Isaiah 61:1-3; 194

J

James 1:19-25 116
James 1:21-22 205
James 1:23-24 204
James 2:1-7 207
James 2:8 207
James 4:4-5 203

Jeremiah 16:1-21 239
Jeremiah 17:14 101
Jeremiah 29:11 185
John 1: 11-14 118
John 10:9 102
John 10:9-11 172
John 11:26 153
John 14:6-10 39
John 20:23 131
John 3:14-18 243
John 9:2 219
John 9:2-5 218
John 9:4 .... 217, 218
John 9:4-5 220
John 9:6-7 219

L

Luke 1:30-33 189
Luke 10:18 118
Luke 11:20 192
Luke 3:31 190
Luke 4:16-20 188
Luke 4:18-19 .... 22, 128
Luke 4:18-21 194
Luke 4:21 188
Luke 7:22-23 141

M

Mark 14:23-27 157
Mark 16:16 102
Mark 16:2 182
Mark 16:20 198
Mark 4:36-41 156
Matthew 1:20-21 190
Matthew 1:21 221
Matthew 10:14 175

Matthew 10:7-8 154
Matthew 16:19 130
Matthew 22:37-40 46
Matthew 24:36-39 222
Matthew 28:18 135
Matthew 28:18-20.119, 135, 141
Matthew 6:19-21 163
Micah 6:8 215

N

Numbers 10:9 101

P

Philippians 4:6-8 65
Proverbs 18:10 103
Proverbs 22:1 94
Proverbs 28:18 102
Psalm 106:8 99
Psalm 109:4 ....13, 226
Psalm 113:1 97
Psalm 118:10 99
Psalm 119:55 100
Psalm 119:89 107
Psalm 124:8 100
Psalm 135:13 100
Psalm 140:13 105
Psalm 20:1 98
Psalm 29:5-8 109
Psalm 3:4-8 90
Psalm 43:3 57
Psalm 44:5 98
Psalm 5:11 98

Psalm 59:13 149
Psalm 61:3 103
Psalm 66:1-4 75
Psalm 68:4 97
Psalm 69: 34-36 6
Psalm 74:21 98
Psalm 75:1 98
Psalm 79:9 99
Psalm 80:19 101
Psalm 80:3 101
Psalm 80:7 101
Psalm 83:18 99
Psalm 9:10 98
Psalm 91:14. 99

R

Revelation 19:1 194
Revelation 19:7 165
Revelation 21: 9-10 24
Revelation 22:17 ...... 11, 199
Romans 1:16-17 169
Romans 10: 12-15 241
Romans 10:10 248
Romans 10:14 96
Romans 12:1-2 211
Romans 12:16-18 214
Romans 12:3-5 212
Romans 12:6-8 213
Romans 12:9-15 213
Romans 6:14 155
Romans 6:23 227
Romans 6:9 153
Romans 8:1-4 206

ABOUT THE AUTHOR

Presently, Jeanne Metcalf serves in the capacity of an ordained minister, working as the Senior Pastor of a ministry, named *"Forward March!"* Ministries. FMM is a part of a global grassroots movement of the Holy Spirit to return Christianity to its New Testament roots. Its primary goals include teaching early church concepts, spreading the gospel, and discipling believers so that all can walk in New Testament power, equipped to turn the world upside down with the impact of the gospel.

Jeanne gained credibility as a gifted teacher, writer, and speaker as she led FMM. With her passion for souls, a God-given insight and love for the Word of God, Rev. Jeanne presents sound biblical teachings on both the Hebraic and Apostolic scriptures, with clarity and simplicity, in a refreshing straightforward format. Those who study the Bible with Jeanne, highly recommend her studies.

Transformed lives stand as witnesses as through Rev. Jeanne's leadership, believers stand equipped, steadfast in their faith, prepared to live it out triumphantly.

CONTACT INFORMATION
*For more great books or
to contact Jeanne, go to*
www.cegullahpublishing.ca

www.ingramcontent.com/pod-product-compliance
Lightning Source LLC
Chambersburg PA
CBHW071621170426
43195CB00038B/1587